A History of the BRITANNIA BUILDING SOCIETY 1856–1985

A History of the BRITANNIA BUILDING SOCIETY

1856–1985

Richard Redden MA (Oxon)

Franey & Co Ltd

Published by Franey & Co Ltd
7 Swallow Place (off Princes Street), London W1R 8AB

ISBN 0 900 382 00 7
Printed by Chandlers (Printers) Ltd
Bexhill-on-Sea, East Sussex

Contents

Foreword

THIS IS THE FIRST history in book form of Britannia in its 128-year history. Two booklets were published to celebrate the 50-year and 100-year anniversaries of the Leek and Moorlands society. The first was written by Thomas Shaw who led the Leek and Moorlands for 57 years from its foundation. The second was a general centenary booklet. This book draws extensively on those accounts and on recent research by Leslie Beardmore, the former deputy general manager of Britannia. Leslie joined the society in 1926 and is one of only four people still alive who were at the old Leek and Moorlands when Hubert Newton arrived in 1933 as secretary — the others are Mrs Dorothy Mathewson who still lives in Leek, Bob Johnson, now in Canada, and Harry Leonard who lives in Brighton.

This book is timed to coincide with Sir Hubert's retirement as chairman after 51 years of service. Sir Hubert has led such an active life and been involved in so many activities in and outside the building society movement, that it has been impossible to mention them all in what is a history of one society, Britannia. But this book nevertheless carries a strong element of biography as it inevitably must. Sir Hubert's chairmanship of The Building Societies Association and presidency of the International Union of Building Societies and Savings and Loans Organisations gave national and international prominence to the Leek and Moorlands besides leaving lasting and affectionate memories within the wider building society movement.

In his 80s, Sir Hubert still retains the kindliness and good humour that have won him that affection. In my own case, it even extended to his taking me to see his beloved Stoke City F.C. on the dreadful day in the 1984-85 season that they first plunged to bottom place in the First Division.

So much of Sir Hubert's career has been spent fighting battles against government and the building society establishment itself that I have necessarily included a large amount of national background in this book. I have drawn extensively on two histories of the movement produced by Franeys — Building Societies, Their Origin and History, by Seymour J. Price, and The Building Society Story, by Herbert Ashworth. I am also grateful to the Building Societies Gazette for letting me look over many volumes of past years and to the Financial Times Business Information Service who supplied much useful information on post-war years.

Richard Redden, April 1985

1: Britannia the Name, Leek the Town

BRITAIN'S BUILDING SOCIETIES still retain the strong local origins that saw them come into existence in the 19th century. Unlike the big banks, most of our biggest societies are still based in the provinces outside London.

Britannia Building Society is one of the country's biggest. It has the most national name of all the building societies. But it still resides in the town from which it sprang — Leek in the Staffordshire moorlands. It began life there as the Leek and Moorlands Permanent Benefit Building Society on May 30, 1856. In a long and eventful history, it has changed name several times as it merged with other societies. But the name of the Staffordshire town remained in its title until 1975 when it became Britannia.

The change of name symbolised the progress of the building society into a national institution. But it was also symbolic of the town of Leek. For Leek people regard their moorland town as the centre of England whatever other geographical claimants there may be to the title.

Britannia is a name that dates from before Roman times and the town of Leek itself dates back deep into history. It is on the route of the old Roman road from Buxton to Chesterton and the first evidence of settlement in this moorland area dates from that time at nearby Abbey Green. Weapons of Briton and Roman origin have also been found in the area.

What of the name Britannia itself? The Romans called our island Britannia but they didn't invent the name. It was the Greeks who did so and it was mentioned in the writings of Aristotle. The exact derivation is unclear. Some scholars argue that the name was derived from the Celtic "bruit-tan", meaning "tin country", a reference to the Cornish tin mines. Others say it came from "Prydain", who was supposed to have been an ancient tribal leader.

As our island faced a succession of invasions and changes in its boundaries, so the Greek name remained as a general expression for it. Over the centuries, Britannia came to mean the spirit of the land. Unlike many countries, the British have come to see this spirit in the form of a mother figure and not a father. And so the female figure we know as Britannia evolved. We know that King Alfred referred to the spirit of Britannia when summoning his men. And as our seafaring and naval traditions developed, so Britannia became also a symbol of the seas surrounding and protecting us.

We know her from our old penny coins and the modern 50p coin as a figure complete with helmet, trident and shield. The origin of that picture comes from Miss Frances Theresa Stewart, later the Duchess of Richmond, in the mid-17th century. At that time, the fashion in court circles was to spend a lot of time dressing up as classical characters. Miss Stewart dressed up as the Roman goddess Minerva, and Sir Peter Lely painted her portrait, where it hangs to this day in the Richmond family seat at Goodwood House. King Charles II himself was fond of Miss Stewart and of her portrait. It was he who ordered it to be reproduced, first on a medal and then on the coins of the realm.

The story of Britannia as a national symbol was completed in 1740 when James Thomson composed a masque about the feats of King Alfred and included the words: "Rule, Britannia, rule the waves; Britons never will be slaves." The words, of course, have undergone a slight modification over the centuries.

Britannia has been the name for battleships, railway engines, aeroplanes, cars, and for the famous Robert Stephenson bridge over the Menai Straits. Now it is the name of one of Britain's largest and most historic building societies.

Britannia Building Society came into being after a history spanning 47 mergers and two previous major changes of name — to the Leek and Westbourne in 1966 and to the Leek, Westbourne and Eastern Counties in 1974. It was not just the name and its romance that appealed. It arose from the desire of the society and its chairman, Sir Hubert Newton, to make itself identifiably British so that it could operate as such — when permitted — inside the European Economic Community. Although that European goal has yet to be achieved today, the figure of Britannia sits resplendent on the brochures and literature of the society, complete not only with shield and trident, but also with the British bulldog.

When the Leek and Moorlands Permanent Benefit Building Society completed its first year of existence in 1857, it had just £3,000 of assets. Three years after the name Britannia came into existence, the assets passed the £1,000 million mark, making it the ninth largest building society in Britain. At the end of 1984, assets were £2,847 million, putting it in eleventh position. The number of borrowers totalled

174,339 and the number of savers 1,325,482.

The headquarters of Britannia are now in a modern building on the outskirts of Leek, named Newton House after Sir Hubert Newton who joined the society in 1933 and led it as secretary, general manager, managing director and chairman into its present leading position in the building society world.

Of all the major building societies — taking the top 20 in 1984 — none is based in so small a town as Leek, which has a population of just 19,700. The big non-London societies are based in much bigger cities such as Halifax, Leeds, Bradford, Leicester, Bristol and Coventry. In fact, there is a second Leek society, completely independent of Britannia — the Leek United and Midlands, founded just seven years afterwards in 1863. It remains a prosperous although a smaller and more localised society.

It is to Britannia's achievement and credit that it has flourished in such a typically small English town as Leek.

The character of Leek fits in with the new name of the society. Occupying a position some 600 feet above sea level at the head of the Churnet River valley in North Staffordshire, it is often described as the "Queen of the Moorlands". It is surrounded by some of the finest hill, moor and dale scenery to be found in the Midlands of England, and the town's history reflects much of the history of the country itself. In Saxon times, it was in the possession of Earl Algar, son of the famous Lady Godiva, and of Leofric, Duke of Mercia. It is recorded in the Domesday book under the name "Lec". The founding and growth of the Leek and Moorlands Permanent Benefit Building Society derives from the major industrial prosperity and development the town enjoyed in the 19th century.

The foundations of that prosperity began in the 18th century as the town changed character from a simple market town to a centre for the spinning, weaving and dyeing of silk and wool.

James Brindley, the canal builder, started in business in the town as a millwright and later died there in 1772 from an illness he is believed to have contracted while surveying the Leek to Froghall Canal. The mill still stands and can be visited by the public.

By 1831, the population had grown to 6,374 and the people were chiefly employed in the silk industry, making ribbons, thrown silk, handkerchiefs, ferrets and galloons. Button manufacture and the making of cotton goods was also carried on. Lead, copper and coal were all mined in the locality.

It was from this environment, in which people were beginning to amass the wealth to save and to want to buy houses, that the Leek and Moorlands Permanent Benefit Building Society grew. But there were two building societies recorded in existence in Leek before it. The first was the Leek Building Society whose plans were set forth in an agreement dated February 5, 1824. Twenty-six years later, in 1850, another building society is recorded, the Leek Benefit Society, certified on April 3, 1850.

Both of these were so-called "terminating societies" whose existence finished when the members who had clubbed together were able to complete the purchase and final ownership of their properties. Their success paved the way for the first permanent society in the town, the Leek and Moorlands, in 1856.

Just one year before, the town had received its first organised form of local government when under the Leek Improvement Act of 1855, it was placed under the administration of Improvement Commissioners. They were replaced by an urban district council in 1894. In the local government reforms of 1974, the council was incorporated into the new Staffordshire Moorlands District of which Leek is the administrative centre. A separate Leek Town Council for town affairs was also created in 1974. The society's former headquarters building in Stockwell Street, New Stockwell House, now forms part of the offices of the Staffordshire Moorlands District Council.

The character of the Leek is not only made by its moorland surroundings but by its architecture, the product of a Victorian father and son. William Sugden and his son, William Larner Sugden, between them monopolised public and private building in the town throughout the last third of the 19th century. William started his practice in 1849 and was joined by his son in 1881. He died in 1892 and his son nine years later.

Now, of course, Leek has undergone much 20th century change although it still retains its old market place complete with stone sets. As Britannia's great rival, the Halifax, once generously remarked, it can justly be called the premier building society town of England. Perhaps the wisdom of its Victorian forefathers in foreseeing the importance of home ownership can be summed up in another Staffordshire saying — "in Staffordshire, mugs are made, not born."

2: Origins of the Leek

THE ORIGINS OF THE building society movement go back to the friendly societies which originated in the late 17th century and grew rapidly in number after 1750. Their members consisted of the workpeople in the growing towns who found themselves divorced from the informal but strong help in distress they and their ancestors had found in rural communities. In the absence of a welfare state, they had to meet the threat to them and their families of illness and injury.

The friendly societies were mutual associations taking in contributions from their members to pay out in the event of ill-health or in case of other necessity, such as the expense arising from a death in the family.

At the end of the 18th century, there were an estimated 7,000 of these societies, along with sickness and burial clubs, savings groups and other self-help organisations such as the money clubs into which members paid a sum each week and balloted for the right to a loan of the week's proceeds.

The friendly societies received their first official recognition in the Friendly Societies Act of 1793 which gave their members proper legal protection.

From the idea of the friendly society, it was but a short step in conception to the idea of a mutual association for the building of homes. The earliest building society is thought to have been established in Birmingham in about 1775. It was called the Ketley's Building Society and took its name from a Mr Ketley, landlord of the Golden Cross Inn where the members met. It was common for the self-help societies to base themselves on a local centre of the community such as the inn. Several other societies are known to have existed in the Birmingham area between 1775 to 1781 and the movement began to grow quickly as the 18th century neared its close.

It was in the Midlands and the North of England that most of the societies sprang up. Population began to shift to these areas as the Industrial Revolution took hold. Records show that some 70 societies were formed between 1775 and 1825, and there must have been many more that went unrecorded.

These first building societies were different in concept from those of modern times. They were essentially building clubs. Their purpose was to raise money so their members could in turn build houses for ownership. When the members all possessed their houses, and had paid off all debt, the societies were dissolved. They were called "terminating societies".

Evidence of such societies usually consists only of notices in contemporary news-sheets. Documents were scarce because those first pioneers had a small membership and a limited timespan of existence.

The terminating societies were entirely local in their activities and average membership seems to have been around the 20 mark. The members lived in the same area and only houses on local sites were built out of the funds.

The houses were built as quickly as funds allowed and normally allotted to members in an order decided by ballot. Members knew each other closely because they came from the same community and strong bonds were forged between them. Leading citizens consented to act as trustees to help the societies acquire a sound financial footing. Their backing often helped societies to borrow money from banks to meet temporary shortages of cash.

It was in this kind of environment that the first recorded building society in Leek came into existence — the Leek Building Society whose plans were set forth in an agreement dated 5th February, 1824.

The plans show that shares were to be paid for by monthly subscriptions of one guinea for six years. For each share, a house valued at £80 was to be acquired. As 42 shares were taken up by the 31 members, some of them would, it seems, have acquired more than one house. With 42 subscriptions of a guinea coming in every month, the society was in the position of being able to finance houses at the rate of one every two months. The houses were built on Ball Haye Green, Leek, which became known as Club Row, a name reflecting the club-like co-operation of the members.

What is important about this first Leek society is the bonds it established between men interested in the finance and building of houses. Because of these bonds, direct links can be seen between this first society and the Leek and Moorlands in the family names recorded in the list of members.

Among the pioneers who signed the deed of the Leek Building Society in 1824, were William Challinor, James Challinor, Josiah

Gaunt, James Wardle, William Johnson, Ralph Mountford, Joseph Billing and K. Killmister.

One other terminating society is recorded in Leek before the advent of the Leek and Moorlands. That is the Leek Benefit Building Society, which was promoted by William Challinor and came into existence on 3rd April, 1850.

The trustees were: James Alsop, Thomas Birch, Joshua Brough, Charles Heaton jnr and Robert Hammersley. Other personnel were: treasurer, Samson Gould; solicitor, William Challinor; surveyor, Edwin Heaton; secretary ("pro tem"), Mr Mollatt. There was a committee consisting of George Hammersley, Thomas Johnson, William Wood, George Wolliscroft, Robert Fergyson, Jonathan Cruso and Thomas Shaw.

The names of William Challinor and Thomas Shaw were later to reappear as promoters of the Leek and Moorlands Permanent Benefit Building Society in 1856. So was the name of Mr Mollatt, presumed to be the W. S. Mollatt on the Leek and Moorlands' first list of directors.

The objects of the 1850 society comprised the erection or purchase of dwelling-houses or other real or leasehold estate to be secured by mortgages. The society offered shares of £120, on a monthly subscription of 10s. a share and an entrance fees of 2s.6d. a share. Investors were to receive 5 per cent interest and borrowers were to pay 5 per cent. Working expenses were to be met by quarterly payments added to the subscriptions.

The society was able to terminate two years and four months earlier than the estimated period of 13 years, ten months and 21 days. The members celebrated with a supper at the George Inn, Leek.

Their success was due to the enterprising purchase early in the society's career and at the personal risk of the trustees and committee, of land in Leek laid out in building plots. This realised considerable profit which was distributed among the members. The area forms the site of Alsop Street, Westwood Terrace and St. George's Row.

In these years, there was an abortive attempt to form a third terminating society in Leek. The society's name was to be The Leek and North Staffordshire Benefit Building and Investment Society. A prospectus for the society shows that its rules and regulations were approved at a meeting at the Town Hall, Leek, on 19th December, 1846. The paper bears the name of George Sawkins, a solicitor then in practice in Leek.

The shares were £120 each and the monthly subscription 10s. 3d., with an entrance fee of 2s. 6d. per share. The names of the directors and other officers were not stated, except that applications for shares were to be made to Mr G. A. Smith, secretary *pro tem,* Ball Haye Street, Leek.

The society either never commenced business or very shortly ceased to exist. Mr Smith was later recorded as a member of the Leek Benefit Building Society on its founding.

By 1850, the idea of the simple terminating society was already dying. Societies were giving up the idea of direct building of houses. It was easier to accumulate funds as part of a general saving scheme and then make advances to members seeking to build or buy their houses.

This method avoided many of the problems faced by the terminating societies — defaulting contractors, shoddy workmanship, delays in construction. It also avoided the inherent disadvantage of the terminating society that not all the houses could be built at the same time. When there were intervals in the building of houses, all sorts of grievances quickly arose over fair treatment for all members.

The first legislation designed specifically to protect and regulate building societies was passed in 1836 and provided the framework within which building societies were to develop into the permanent institutions we know today.

In the first quarter of the 19th century, a few building societies had registered as friendly societies under the 1793 Act. But the remainder had no clear legal standing. It was a dispute in 1835 over a proposed change in the law to make building society shares liable to stamp duty which led to the 1836 Act.

By 1835, there were societies in many parts of the country and some towns had several. The proposal to make shares liable to duty was a very serious one. For members who found they could not keep up the subscription, the escape avenue was the transfer of shares to someone else wanting to become a member. The stamp duty, if enacted, might well have posed a serious deterrent to those wanting to become members.

A delegation of societies from Manchester and Liverpool saw the Chancellor of the Exchequer, Thomas Spring Rice, to put their case. Rice agreed with them and decided as a consequence that the societies should be protected by a special Act of Parliament.

The 1836 Act turned out to be badly drafted. It was later to lead to a number of disputes over the meaning of its clauses. But it conferred substantial benefits on the societies. They were not only exempted from the stamp duty. They were also exempted from the usury laws of the time. And mortgages could now be discharged by a receipt from the

Board of Directors and Chief General Manager, January 1985.
Back row, left to right: F. M. Shaw (Chief General Manager), N. Cowburn, D. Berriman, John Hill, S. J. Sebire.
Front row, left to right: The Hon. P. A. Strutt, MC, John Quipp (Deputy Chairman), Sir Hubert Newton (Chairman), E. W. Wallaker, The Earl of Shrewsbury and Waterford.

Sir Hubert Newton, Hon MA (Keele), FCIS, FCBSI, President 1985-, Chairman 1964-1965, 1966-1974, 1976-1985, Managing Director 1962-1969, Director 1938-1985, General Manager 1941-1965, Secretary 1933-1963.

Building Society

The Chief Office in Leek.

John Quipp, ACBSI, Chairman 1985-, Deputy Chairman 1983-85, Managing Director, 1980-1981 (Deputy, 1977-80), Director 1977-, General Manager 1970-1976.

Norman Cowburn, FCIS, FCBSI, Managing Director 1977-1984, Director 1977-, Chief General Manager 1970-1976, General Manager 1966-1970, Secretary 1963-1965.

trustees, doing away with the previous requirement for a deed of reconveyance. This represented a considerable saving. In 1846, the Chief Registrar of Friendly Societies was to become the certifying officer for building societies as well, overseeing the provisions of the 1836 Act.

The 1836 Act stimulated the growth of the movement, and by the time the Leek Benefit Society came into existence in 1850, there were about 1,500 active societies. By 1850, many terminating societies were anticipating in their structure the growth of the permanent movement. Many had two different kinds of subscribers — those who invested to borrow and those who simply invested. The latter were savers only and not paid-up shareholders.

The size of societies was increasing too. Numbers were sometimes as high as 100 in the 1830s and some societies were known to have as many as 250 members in the 1850s.

The Victorian actuary, Arthur Scratchley, claimed to be the man who created the concept of the permanent society. Scratchley acted as adviser to many societies on tables of repayment. He wrote the standard mid-19th-century work on the principles of operation of building societies, and it was in later editions of this work that he claimed the idea of the permanent society as his. But a rival claimant was another actuary, J. H. James, who advocated the idea in a pamphlet published in 1845. Whatever the conflicting claims, it was certainly Scratchley who had a major influence on the development of the permanent society.

Scratchley was to give advice to the founders of the Leek and Moorlands on the prospectus setting up their own society. He founded a permanent society himself, the London & Metropolitan Counties, in 1848. But there are records of permanent societies in existence in 1845 and 1846 — two in London and four in the provinces.

So by the time the Leek and Moorlands Permanent Benefit Building Society was formed in 1856, the idea of the permanent society was well established, even though it met some resistance from the Northern societies who clung to the idea that each member should become a houseowner.

The Leek and Moorlands was a natural consequence of the success of the Leek Benefit society. The promoters of the new society which took office at No. 1 Stockwell Street, Leek, were the solicitors of the Leek Benefit which had five more years to run until its demise.

The solicitors were William Challinor, William B. Badnall and Joseph Challinor. Their managing clerk, Thomas Shaw, was chosen as secretary of the new society.

Shaw later became a partner in the firm of solicitors who were called Challinors and Shaw. They remained the head office solicitors to the Leek and Moorlands throughout its existence. Shaw became a director of the Leek and Moorlands, ex officio, as secretary, although his name was not among the members of the board recorded in the first annual report in 1857.

Shaw gave up the secretaryship in 1869, on being elected by his co-directors to the new post of managing director, which he held until his death in 1913. He was to lead the society in the growth which took it to a position among Britain's leading building societies by the turn of the century.

The prospectus for the new society contained the following description of its proposed activities:

Objects:

1. To advance money to its Members at a trifling expense for periods of five, seven, ten, twelve, fourteen or twenty-one years (repayable by monthly instalments), to enable them to purchase houses or land, or build houses for their own occupation, or for letting, or to pay off mortgages, or for any other purposes.

2. To enable Members engaged in mining or agricultural pursuits to borrow money on their leaseholds, with proper security, so as to erect buildings, or permanent works, or to provide for the fines payable on renewal of their leases.

3. To enable those Members who do not wish to purchase, or build, or borrow, to obtain a much higher rate of interest for their money than is paid by an ordinary Savings Bank, on security equally good and available.

Advantages and Features:

1. The Society being a permanent one, members may enter at any time, either as Investors or Borrowers, without being required to pay any arrears of subscriptions or increased entrance fees.

2. The Subscriptions on Investing Shares of £25 each, are 2s. 3d. per month, for 14 years only, at the end of which period the shares of each Member are paid out with compound interest, and also a proportion of the profits to be made; any number of shares may be taken.

3. Members can withdraw (after the first year) on giving notice, and receive back their monthly subscriptions with compound interest, or may sell and transfer their shares at any time.

4. Advances are made to Members to the full amount of their shares,

repayable with moderate interest, by fixed monthly instalments, during five, seven, ten, twelve, fourteen or twenty-one years, to suit the convenience and circumstances of the Members.

5. Mortgages to the Society may be redeemed at any time on payment of the value of future subscriptions for the unexpired period of the loan term.

6. Persons in all ranks of life, including Married Women and Minors, are admitted. No extras for working expenses.

Scratchley, writing from "The Friendly Societies Institute" in Pall Mall, London, on 26th May, 1856, certified that "the Rules and Rates of the 'Leek and Moorlands Permanent Benefit Building Society' are founded upon equitable and sound principles, and may be safely adopted for its use."

The rules and Scratchley's Certificate were sent to the official Registrar immediately after Scratchley's reply. On 30th May, the Registrar issued his certificate declaring the rules conformed with the law.

The first meeting of the new society was held on 2nd June. Shaw in a jubilee pamphlet he wrote 50 years later in 1906, recalled the meeting as follows: "Upwards of 120 persons enrolled themselves as Members, and many shares were subscribed for. After stating the objects and advantages of the Society, Members were with a view of encouraging thrift advised in the Prospectus, if they did not wish to build or purchase houses, and so become their own landlords, to save money on which they would obtain interest and profits."

This last provision anticipated the savings function of the building society movement that was to follow. The names of the trustees and others associated with the project, were listed with the rules, presumably to impress investors with the fact that the society was eminently sound and respectable.

Several of these personalities were among those mentioned in the records of terminating societies.

The first volume in a carefully preserved complete set of the society's minute books, covers the period from 6th June, 1856, to 18th June, 1867. The directors are recorded as having held their first meeting at the offices of their solicitors in Stockwell Street, Leek. George Hammersley was chosen as the first head of the society, being given the dual titles of president and chairman. The meeting had to decide which directors were to retire after one year, and which after two. The names of the directors were written on slips of paper and drawn out of a hat.

Other business included the appointment of a committee of directors to consider applications for loans. This Loan Committee remained for many years a feature of the board's structure. Another committee was elected to look after publicity. Its particular task was to hold meetings in the area "to explain the objects of the Society and obtain members".

Among the resolutions agreed was one that "a Prospectus be prepared, and 1,000 copies printed and circulated — and that a short prospectus be advertised once in the Staffordshire Advertiser, and Stafford Sentinel Papers". The "printing, etc., as to the Society" was to be "divided among such of the Printers, etc., as are members".

The first application was considered for a loan — but not the first to be granted. It came from the Rev. John Sneyd, and was referred to the Loan Committee.

The first meeting of the Loan Committee came on 20th June, 1856. It "resolved that the application by Mr James Mycock for an advance of four shares for the 21 years term be accepted and agreed to, and that the money be advanced on the Security being completed". It was the Rev. Sneyd's turn on 30th June. The Loan Committee agreed to an advance of £500 "following the report of Surveyors". It was also "resolved that Mr Nall's offer to advance £100 at £4½ per cent and Mr Challinor's offer to lend £150 at £4½ per cent and Banker's commission, to enable the Society to meet its engagements to Mr Sneyd be accepted, and that the Treasurer be requested to give Mr Challinor a memorandum for the amount".

As Mr Nall was the society's treasurer and also chairman of the Loan Committee, and Mr Challinor the solicitor, there should have been no problems with this arrangement which was a fairly common procedure with small societies which had wealthy directors.

A board meeting on 14th July, 1856, noted that since the start of operations, the society's receipts amounted to £322 19s. 5d. and that the treasurer had a balance in hand of £34 19s. 5d. The directors agreed to allow £4 per cent discount on subscriptions paid in advance up to two years, and £3 10s. 0d. per cent for longer periods. One of the directors, Peter Magnier, Jnr, who had resigned, was replaced by William Sugden, a local surveyor.

At the end of the first year, the directors presented "with satisfaction" the first annual report and balance sheet. Income from all sources amounted to £3,201 11s. 2d., of which £3,000 had been advanced to members "on Mortgage of approved freehold property", suggesting that the demand for the society's services had allowed the directors to choose among would-be borrowers. The prospectus had not limited advances to freehold property.

Subscriptions paid out and discount and interest allowed or paid amounted to £9 15s. 7d. The whole of the expenses for the formation of the society and its management during the year, including the fees paid to Scratchley and the Registrar, the printing of the rules, posters and prospectuses, and the secretary and stewards' salaries, came to just £86 19s. 10d., leaving a balance in hand at the end of the year of £104 15s. 9d.

At the close of the first year, the society had 203 members as investors and borrowers. The investors held 1,186 shares and the borrowers 120, making a total of 1,306 shares.

The directors added that they, "being fully convinced of the great utility of Societies of this description to nearly all classes as affording advantages of borrowing and repaying which cannot elsewhere be obtained, congratulate the members that this their first and therefore most trying year, has produced so satisfactory a result, and they look upon it as an earnest of still greater success in succeeding years, when a larger number of members may reasonably be expected and the expenses of management thereby considerably lessened in proportion to the number of shares".

The directors were also "pleased to observe that not only the working classes, but the more wealthy avail themselves of the advantages offered by the Society, and feel satisfied that as persons become better acquainted with its principles, the more extended will be its business, and the larger in proportion will be its profits".

The directors were too optimistic about their most trying time being behind them. The society experienced a slowing down in its second year, and as with all societies, was often to suffer the swings and roundabouts of changing economic conditions.

The Annual Report and Accounts dated 24th May, 1858, did show a profit of £105 compared with £85 in the first year. But the directors regretted that "owing to the depression in trade, some of the Members were compelled to avail themselves of their powers to withdraw their Shares; but at the same time feel pleased that by means of the Society they had to some extent provided against such an event, which many of them remarked they should not otherwise have done".

The directors added: "It is also worthy of observation that there was not a single arrear of repayment subscription at the close of the year, a fact which proves that the money has been judiciously invested".

The increase in profit was misleading because the first year's profit was only struck after the naturally heavy expenses of formation. In the directors' words, the expenses were "of considerable amount attending the formation of the Society" and "would not recur again".

The total of the initial expenses was £86 19s. 10d., which might sound modest enough to modern ears. It included a "Tin Box for Deeds Painting and Lettering", 18s. 8d.; "Bill Posters, Postage and Sundries", £5 17s. 6d.; "Firing, Gas, etc., on Subscription nights, etc.", £3 3s. 0d.; "Salaries: Secretary, £25; Two Stewards, £6 6s. 0d.; Agent at Ipstones, £1 1s. 0d."

The second year's expenses totalled £46, including £3 7s. 0d. for "a cupboard for Books, Papers, etc".

Arthur Scratchley continued as actuary to the society. At the end of the fifth year, he investigated the business and reported that everything was in order. The books showed a clear surplus of £1,173, from which the directors set aside £359 as a Reserve Fund and divided the remainder as a bonus to shareholders.

Profits in later years were helped considerably by some of the directors and trustees buying land in Leek at their own risk.

This was in 1882, when they acquired land lying between Derby Street, Stockwell Street, and Market Street. They gave up to the town voluntarily two cottages, a stable and land on the south side of Stockwell Street, which enabled the then Leek Improvement Commissioners to widen and raise Stockwell Street between Union Street and Ball Haye Street.

The directors and trustees formed Bath Street and Ford Street, and laid out the property in lots. The lots were ultimately sold off, with the large profits on the deals coming to the society.

The land given to the town was almost opposite the site of what was later to be the chief office of the Leek and Moorlands, New Stockwell House, opened in 1937, and its predecessor, No. 15 Stockwell Street, opened in 1895 when the original offices at No. 1 Stockwell Street were given up.

In 1863, it was decided to end the financial year on 31st December instead of 31st May, and this was done in 1864 when the accounts covered the whole period from 31st May, 1863, to 31st December, 1864.

In the late 1860s and through the 1870s, the society's business spread into neighbouring areas. Many of the minutes of the board concern members or applicants for loans, in Derbyshire and the Potteries. In the Potteries, quite a number of "beerhouses" figured in mortgage business.

As early as 1867, the Loan Committee dealt with an application from a man in Cornwall, Thomas Miners, Mine Agent, of Redruth, for an advance of £750 on the security of houses in Croydon.

On 10th January, 1877, the Loan Committee agreed to advance the surprisingly large sum of £15,000 to an applicant who had asked for £16,000 on 126 houses or cottages at Cobridge in Staffordshire. The interest charged was six per cent, falling to five per cent. A report on the property from John Brealey, director and surveyor, and and another report from the solicitors were considered. The solicitors had examined the title to the property and "a reservation as to minerals".

It was not just in such large lending on landlord ownership that the society differed from the building societies of today. As the society's objects made clear, it was free to indulge in commercial lending. It financed farm property and dye and pottery works as well as homes.

What is clear from the records is that the society's transactions were sometimes bolder than any which a modern building society would undertake. But this is not to cast doubt on the integrity and viability of the Leek and Moorlands society of those days. Such speculative deals were characteristic of the time. The deals were shrewd ones and usually at the personal risk of trustees and some directors.

The minutes show a clear appreciation of the need for security as a basic principle of building society lending. For example, in April, 1866, the Loan Committee with John Brealey in the chair, considered an application from the Rev. James Badnall for an advance of shares representing £200, "to be secured by the covenant of his Uncle John Cruso, Esq, in addition to his own". The committee declined to grant it "because of the rules restricting the Society from lending on any other than real security", even though the applicant was evidently a respectable person and probably a relative of one of the partners on the firm of Challinor, Badnall and Challinor, the solicitors.

It should be added that the Leek and Moorlands was helped in these formative years by a generally favourable economic background. This was a period of steadily rising commodity prices and property values.

Building societies were now an accepted part of the nation's financial life although other institutions such as savings banks were also growing quickly. The Post Office itself entered the market for small savings in 1863. In 1859, that Victorian apostle of self-help, Samuel Smiles, published his famous work "Self Help" extolling the values of thrift. Smiles was a strong supporter of the building societies. Five years later in a public speech, he painted this picture of the movement: "The accumulation of property has the effect which it always has on thrifty men; it makes them steady, sober and diligent. It weans them from revolutionary notions and makes them conservative. When working men, their industry and frugality, have secured their own independence, they will cease to regard the sight of others' well-being as a wrong inflicted on themselves; and it will no longer be possible to make political capital out of their imaginary woes . . . Building societies are on the whole amongst the most excellent methods of illustrating the advantages of thrift".

These years of growth for permanent building societies were examined by the Royal Commission on Friendly Societies set up in 1872 and which included the building societies in its terms of reference. By this time, it was clear that the 1836 Act was inadequate to regulate properly the burgeoning activities of the building society movement. The law was uncertain over the borrowing powers of societies. That power was questioned a number of times in legal cases.

For a time in the 1850s, the Chief Registrar would only approve a rule which required trustees to give their personal security for loans taken out. Later the situation worsened further, and the Registrar refused to certify any proposed borrowing rules. It was not until a test case was brought in 1868 that the right to borrow was definitely established.

Other issues such as the conditions in which a building society could be wound up and the redemption of mortgages were also shrouded in legal obscurity.

The Commission found that the permanent societies had been judiciously managed. Failures of building societies which had been common in the days of terminating societies alone, were now rare. The societies were promoting the investment of several million pounds yearly in property and "had a great influence in training the working classes in business habits".

The Commission stated that exemption from stamp duties was not of vital importance to building societies and not justifiable from the public point of view. They recommended that mortgages up to £200 only should be exempt. Societies should continue to be registered with the Registrar of Friendly Societies and the Registrar should have discretion to disallow provisions of an inequitable nature when he certified society rules.

The Commission's report was the background and stimulus to the 1874 Building Societies Act, the first of two late Victorian pieces of legislation to govern the conduct of the industry.

By this time, Shaw had become the first managing director of the Leek and Moorlands. He had resigned as secretary in August, 1869, and William Brough was appointed in his place. Shaw was presented with a gold watch and chain and clock, and bronze figures, paid for from money voluntarily subscribed by members. The presentation took place at a supper at the Swan Inn in Leek, on 30th June, 1870.

The month of June 1870 marked a milestone for the society, for a large number of the shares became paid up for the first time since subscriptions on them were started in 1856. This meant that the members now became entitled to withdraw the full amount of their shares of £25 each with the bonuses which had been added out of profits.

The report and balance sheet showed that £4429 5s. 5d. had been allotted in bonuses. Of this, £1042 12s. 0d. was actually paid out, leaving a surplus of £3245 0s. 9d. after providing for liabilities. From the surplus, £1779 9s. 0d. was allocated for bonuses, and the residue of £1465 11s. 9d. was set aside as a reserve fund for future contingencies.

In 1874, Thomas Brealey became the secretary and was to hold the post for 35 years. With Shaw and Brealey in tandem, the path was set for the prosperous years of expansion of the late Victorian era.

3: New Laws, New Times

THOMAS SHAW HANDLED the Leek and Moorlands representations over the Bill leading to the 1874 Act. He exchanged extensive correspondence with MPs and others involved in the passage of the Bill through Parliament.

In spite of this, it was to be five years before the Leek and Moorlands directors sought incorporation under the Act. They wanted to adapt their business slowly to the Act's requirements and test out how the new laws worked in practice. Shaw in his booklet of 1906 simply says they "deemed it prudent" to see how the new Act worked, although he admitted it "conferred many additional facilities" on building societies.

Five years before the legislation, a significant event in the history of the building society movement occurred with the founding in 1869 of the Building Societies Protection Association — now The Building Societies Association. Its brief was to monitor proceedings in Parliament affecting the societies and "to protect and extend their interests, privileges and advantages".

The founding members were a group of societies in the London area and the Leek and Moorlands was not represented at the first meeting. But it was soon to appear in the records of the Association as an active member. At the second annual meeting on 12th May, 1871, the financial statement showed that the Leek and Moorlands was among the subscribers to a special parliamentary fund. The handwritten entry can still be seen in the archives of The Building Societies Association in London. The Leek's first contribution was one of £1 1s., followed by another contribution of £2 2s.

The Association was active in safeguarding the interests of the societies as the legislation went through Parliament. It was not plain sailing and there were some heated exchanges with the Gladstone government. The government wanted legislation which would have put building societies under the Companies Act of 1862.

Since 1870, the Association had made several attempts to get its own legislative proposals through Parliament. This culminated in a Bill from the Association coming before Parliament in March, 1873, based on many of the Royal Commission's proposals, whereupon the Government published its own Bill. This Bill provided that all building societies should become joint stock companies and be subject to the Companies Act.

The protests of the societies were so vehement that the Bill was withdrawn after just eight days. It was reintroduced in a new form and although it dropped the Companies Act requirement, its clauses were still based on the Act. Again the Bill was withdrawn, together with that of the Association.

The Government's view throughout this episode was that the building societies were simply seeking to protect their own position. The societies were not prepared to concede the degree of supervision which friendly societies, co-operative societies and provident societies underwent.

It took a change of government to break the deadlock. On 26th January, 1874, Gladstone dissolved Parliament several months before the expiry of its full term. The election the next month brought in Disraeli as Prime Minister. His Home Secretary, Assheton Cross, and his Chancellor, Sir Stafford Northcote, were firm supporters of the building societies and the way was clear for legislation on the lines favoured by the societies. The Bill received the Royal Assent in July, 1874. On only one point were the societies disappointed. Their proposed clause exempting themselves from stamp duty was dropped.

The Act was to remain the principle piece of legislation on building societies for the next 100 years. It stipulated 14 items which must be dealt with in the rules of a society, relating to investment of funds, changing of rules, directors' powers, custody of deeds etc.

The liabilities of investing members and borrowers were clearly defined and no incorporated society under the Act was allowed to own land and buildings except for its own offices. A copy of the annual statement of receipts and expenditure had to be sent to the Chief Registrar, and another displayed in the society's offices.

How did the Leek and Moorlands manage to stay out of the Act's provisions for five years? The answer was that while the Act stopped any more societies being set up under the 1836 Act, it gave to existing societies the option of continuing under the 1836 Act or becoming incorporated under the new provisions. So from 1874, there were two kinds of societies that remained non-incorporated. The societies that remained non-incorporated were mostly the old terminating societies so the Leek and Moorlands seems to have been out of line with many of its fellow permanent societies.

The directors at last obtained a certificate under the Act on 31st October, 1879. The certificate was historically significant in another way too. The words "Permanent" and "Benefit" were dropped from the title of the Leek and Moorlands, the first of the name changes the society was to undergo.

On the 29th December, 1879, the Chief Registrar certified the incorporated society formally after examining the new rules that had been drawn up.

The changes meant that it was now possible to appeal to investors who did not intend to borrow, a policy which had been embodied in the original prospectus. The new rules also brought preference shares into the society's structure. Such shares could now be issued and money on deposit could be received at a rate of interest lower than for ordinary members' shares because of the preferential legal claim to repayment.

Looking at the societies' accounts for the intervening five years, a big drop in advances and a big increase in the Reserve Fund can be noticed. The totals are (1874 figure first, 1879 figures in brackets): Income £53,600 (£67,000); Advance to borrowers £40,000 (£29,300); Reserve Fund £3,000 (£8,500). The number of members' accounts was not recorded for 1874. The total for 1879 was 1,172.

The 1874 Act provided a period of stability for building societies and it took two decades for some of its obvious deficiencies to come home to roost. The Leek society continued to prosper in what were generally good years economically for building societies.

In 1878, a testimonial of a silver ink stand was presented to George Hammersley to mark his 22 years in office as president and chairman. He died the following year on 1st March, 1879. John Ward, a trustee and director of the society since its formation, succeeded him as chairman.

The post of president appears to have lapsed at this time. Like Hammersley, Ward held the chairmanship until his death. He died on 2nd November, 1890. The new chairman was Arthur Nicholson, who was later to be knighted.

It was Nicholson who was instrumental in helping the Leek and Moorlands obtain new headquarters. On 5th April, 1894, he sold a site in Stockwell Street to the society for new offices. The offices were built to designs by John Brealey, brother of Thomas Brealey, and a local architect and surveyor for many years associated with the Leek and Moorlands. They were opened the following year, taking the address of 15 Stockwell Street. It was the first of three moves of headquarters in the society's long history, all occasioned by sustained business expansion. The building remains today and is occupied by the district council. The date of the society's foundation can still be seen above its door.

Soon after the move, a broadsheet was issued by the society in October, 1896, headed: "Money Wanted, Leek and Moorlands Building Society, Established above 40 years". According to the broadsheet, receipts to date were over £1,600,000, annual income about £100,000, and "Reserve Fund invested in Consols and Government Securities over £25,000".

The broadsheet carried a picture of the society's office with the statement above: "This society has no Branches or Agents, and its only Offices are the New Buildings, 15 Stockwell Street, Leek".

What is interesting in the broadsheet is the faith the society placed in its Reserve Fund investments and its sole office as selling points to the would-be investor. To the eyes of later times, these look far less attractive propositions. Government securities could fall as well as rise in value. Risk was lessened if it could be spread over a wider geographical area. As societies found their assets and liabilities growing, the logic of a spread of risk became ever more apparent.

By the time the broadsheet appeared, the first spectacular building society failures were making themselves felt. In 1891, the Portsea Island Society suspended payment when fraud over a number of years by the secretary was revealed. The society was found to have assets of £435,000 against liabilities of £624,000.

But the Portsea was only a relatively localised society like the Leek. The collapse which really stunned the movement was to come a year later, that of the Liberator, the largest society in the country.

This had been set up 25 years before by Jabez Balfour, a clerk who was also a Congregational lay preacher. His religious background enabled him to draw on the support and recommendations of non-conformist ministers around the country. An agency network was built up which pulled in savings from many people who had never considered the idea of investment before.

At first the society operated normally and respectably but then Balfour fell prey to the vaulting ambition his success had fuelled. He started to channel money into building companies and hotel and luxury flat development. He became the MP for Tamworth in 1880, and in 1882 started his own bank.

But his schemes became ever more speculative and began to go spectacularly wrong. His response was cover-up and deception until the whole pack of cards collapsed with over £3 million owing.

Shareholders got nothing and depositors very little. Balfour fled to Argentina but was extradited and jailed for 14 years.

This extraordinary turn of events led to the Building Societies Act, 1894, which placed a battery of fresh controls on the movement and put it under the direct authority of the Chief Registrar of Friendly Societies, whose role had hitherto mainly related to initial certification. He was now given powers to intervene in the affairs of any society if suspicions were aroused. He could in certain circumstances even dissolve the society.

Far more detailed information was demanded of the amounts due on individual mortgages, enabling a society's members to discover whether it was making a high proportion of its loans on large commercial or industrial properties.

The requirement was laid down that one of the auditors had to be an accoutant in public business. The certificate required from the auditors was also strengthened.

Mortgage assets on which borrowing was based were more strictly defined, for example by excluding mortgages upwards of twelve months in arrear.

Shaw and the Leek and Moorlands welcomed the Act for the protection it gave to the movement and its members, and had no qualms about the content. The changes ushered in a period of relative stability just as the 1874 Act had. Another 16 years were to elapse before the next major collapse — that of the Birkbeck Building Society in 1910.

Advertising was widely used for the first time by the societies, as the Leek's broadsheet demonstrated. The importance of the owner occupier as the primary support of the movement was increasingly recognised. Owner occupiers could normally expect a mortgage based on a higher percentage of the value of property than could other clients.

A fundamental advance came in 1895 when the question of income tax liability was settled on a permanent basis by the tax authorities and societies. The modern system was started of the societies paying tax on interest according to an assessment based on the income tax liability of investors as a whole.

The Birkbeck collapse in 1910 came about for fundamentally different reasons from that of the Liberator. The 1894 Act required that unincorporated societies, if set up after 1856, were to become incorporated. But this left out some 60 unincorporated societies which had been set up before 1856. The Birkbeck was one of these and, in fact, the exemption in the 1894 Act was principally for its benefit.

The Birkbeck was set up in 1851. Although registered as a building society, it really functioned as a bank, providing a useful service to poorer people to whom the joint stock banks did not appeal. Most of the society's funds were in Government and Colonial securities and Corporation Stock, in freehold ground rents and cash. It remained unincorporated under the 1894 Act because of the borrowing limitations the Act imposed on incorporated societies.

The Birkbeck was hit by rising interest rates which depressed the value of its stocks and by speculative rumours following the failure of another bank. There was no suggestion of fraud as in the Liberator collapse. But as a bank, the Birkbeck was among the largest in the country and as a building society, it was the largest, with assets of some £12 million before the run on it.

Once again, confidence in the building society movement was severely shaken, although no immediate legislation was to result. The idea of building societies combining a banking function receded.

The minutes of the Leek and Moorlands board meetings right up to the First World War showed little concern with any events outside the locality. In the year of the Birkbeck failure, a characteristic meeting of the board passed what in fact became an annual resolution for some years. This was that the £200 for remuneration of the directors ("free from deduction of Income Tax") should be shared among them according to their attendance at meetings. If they came later or left early, this would count as half an attendance.

The booklet written by Shaw in 1906 listed the 1904 league table of societies with a reserve fund of more than £12,500. The Leek and Moorlands with its fund of £39,465 came ninth out of the 35 societies listed, an impressive indication of the national eminence it had obtained, even though it was still very much a locally-orientated society. As now, Leek stood out as being the smallest town by far to be the home of a major society.

A total of 56 incorporated and three non-incorporated societies were listed in Staffordshire in 1904. The nearest to the Leek and Moorlands in reserve fund terms were the Third Longton Boro' Mutual of Longton, with £15,268, and the Leek United Permanent with £14,491. They held 28th and 32nd positions respectively in the national table. At this time, there were around 2,000 building societies, all locally based — compared to a figure today of just 200.

The 1906 jubilee of the society was marked on 29th June, by a dinner held by Arthur Nicholson at his home at Highfield Hall. Shaw's long years of service which had brought the society to such national eminence, were marked by the presentation of a "massive rose bowl bearing a suitable inscription, two smaller bowls, and two cake stands, all in sterling silver". Shaw in return pointed to the society's progress over the 50 years, which he hoped would be maintained in the years to come.

In 1909, the longstanding secretary, Thomas Brealey, died. He was succeeded by Francis Billing, who had been clerk and accountant to the society since March, 1894. Billing was a Leek man and had gained his first experience in building society work with the Leek United. He had later worked for a local solicitors firm, Hacker and Allen, and then in the town clerk's department in Cardiff. He returned to Leek in 1894 to join the Leek and Moorlands.

Shaw himself died four years later and he was succeeded as managing director by his son, Arthur Hugh Shaw, who had joined the board in 1891. The directors recorded their sorrow at Shaw's death in these words:

"It is with the deepest regret, the Directors record the death of Mr Thomas Shaw, the Managing Director and senior solicitor of the society, which event took place on 30th January, 1913, after an illness of three months. Mr Shaw's connection with the society dates from its formation in May, 1856, upwards of 56 years ago, as a result of steps taken by him in conjunction with the late Messrs W. Challinor, W. B. Badnall and J. Challinor. He was the first secretary and later became and continued to the time of his death, the Managing Director and Solicitor of the Society".

"During the whole of that long period, no important business in connection with the society has been transacted in which he did not take a prominent part. It would be difficult to estimate to what extent the society owes its present position to that sound judgement and kindly interest he was at all times so ready and willing to bestow on matters appertaining to its welfare".

Like his father, Arthur Hugh Shaw was a partner in the firm of Messrs Challinors and Shaw. He was to become a member of The Building Societies Association Executive Committee, and concentrated as a lawyer on helping the Association keep abreast of all legislation affecting the movement's interests. Billing too became a well-known figure at the meetings of the Association.

In 1912, Sir Arthur Nicholson had retired from the board and 100 guineas was spent on a silver presentation plate. He remained a trustee and held the title of president from 1918 until his death at Bournemouth in 1929.

The outbreak of the First World War caused no ruffles to the calm of

Thomas Shaw,
Managing Director 1869-1913,
Director 1856-1913,
Secretary 1856-1869

Henry Salt,
Director 1879-1932,
President 1929-1932

Arthur Hugh Shaw,
Director 1891-1929,
Managing Director 1913-1929

William Hassall, JP, CC,
Director 1907-1938,
Chairman 1934-1938,
President 1934-1938

the society's business as witnessed in its minutes book. The first meeting of the board after the outbreak of war was on 10th August, 1914. The minutes show no hint of the board considering the longer term implications of the war. Presumably, like most of their generation, they assumed it would be over in a short time. The minutes record that they passed a resolution that certain listed applications for loans "be declined mainly owing to the present state of the Society's available funds, having regard to the war crisis".

In August, the bank rate rose to ten per cent and there were fears nationally of widespread withdrawal of building society funds. Although societies tightened up on withdrawal terms, it was soon clear that there was no danger from any loss of public confidence.

In December, the Leek and Moorlands directors discussed the effect of the increase in income tax because of the war, and considered interest rates. They decided on a minimum charge of 4.25 per cent to borrowers. The Managing Director urged that no bonus should be paid to members for 1914, "owing to the great depreciation of the Reserve Fund Investments".

Interestingly, the interest rate move was discussed beforehand by Arthur Shaw and Billing with the Leek United. It is one of the few formally recorded instances of co-operation between the two societies although the informal contacts have been plentiful. A second instance was recorded in September, 1917, when reference is made to a letter from the Leek United, asking the Leek and Moorlands not to advance money at less than five per cent. On the face of it, this seems a strange and peremptory request. The minutes record that "the secretary was instructed to inform them the directors are unable to bind themselves but will endeavour to obtain five per cent in the majority of loans agreed to".

As the war progressed, the building society movement felt the stiff competition from the more competitive rates of interest offered by government war stock. Between 1914 and 1918, total assets of the movement increased only from £66.2 million to £68.5 million. But the societies still found themselves with considerable cash surpluses, which they too invested in war stock, the Leek and Moorlands included, as the minutes show.

In February, 1915, a Special Committee of the Leek and Moorlands board met and recommended measures to deal with mortgage payments in arrears and payments suspended. They agreed that a bonus of 2d. in the £ could be paid for 1914. They also resolved to write down the value of the society's investments.

Obviously the war brought grave problems with mortgage repayments for those called to war service. Of an estimated eight milion homes in the country, about 15 per cent were now owner-occupied. The societies were to gain considerably in public esteem by dealing gently and sympathetically with borrowers hit by the misfortunes of war.

In March, 1915, the Leek and Moorlands minutes show that the board examined the books and noted that the bank balance amounted to over £23,000. The following August, the secretary held £270 in cash and the account at the bank was overdrawn by £84. The cash shortage was remedied by the autumn.

The records indicate that on the whole the society's lending was soundly based. Although the war checked progress, the effect was more than cancelled out in the post-war years. The records show a considerable increase in business in the final year of the war.

The minute books show the many day-to-day transactions that were no different to the many listed in peacetime. The society's heavy lending on agricultural land and on industrial mortgages in the pottery and tile industry appears to go on as normal. Only occasionally, do reminders of the grim war around break out. The Peak Hydro at Buxton is one such reminder.

The society leased out the Hydro and the first wartime reference comes in October, 1915, when a Mr C. Flint Buxton asks for permission to let off the ballroom for cinema performances.

For an unexplained reason, the directors "did not consider it advisable to do so". Then the minutes record the taking over of the Hydro in 1916 by the Canadian Red Cross. On 28th March, 1917, the lease is transferred to the Canadian Medical Service. The transaction is minuted as "underletting the premises to His Majesty the King as represented by the Honourable Ministry of Overseas Forces of Canada, the present lessees remaining responsible for the rent."

Wartime conditions obviously brought trouble to some of the smaller societies. On 11th September, 1916, the North Stafford £50 Permanent Benefit Building Society approaches the Leek and Moorlands to ask it to take the North Stafford over. The North Stafford directors state that "owing to the war, they are only able to keep going with difficulty". The offer is declined although no reason is given. This is the second recorded approach to the Leek and Moorlands by a society asking to be taken over. The first was in 1914 when the Cheadle and District Economic Building Society approached the Leek, although no record of its difficulties is listed. It too was declined. The two episodes provide a sharp contrast to the later eagerness of the Leek to take smaller societies into its fold.

In April, 1916, the question of insurance for aircraft damage is raised in the minutes. It has apparently been included in standard insurance policies for the first time. The "great majority" of borrowers accept but there are some dissenting voices, representing mortgages totalling £30,000. The directors resolve to deal with the matter after the war although not before they have pressed the dissenting borrowers further.

Only once does the terrible human tragedy of the war become apparent. On 9th July, 1917, the directors expressed their sympathy to their fellow director, Edward Keates, "in the anxiety he is undergoing in respect of his son, Fred, who is posted as missing".

The last board meeting of the war fell on Armistice Day, 11th November, 1918. Henry Salt, who had taken over from Sir Arthur Nicholson as chairman in 1912, conducted it.

The books were inspected and the board reported a balance of £84,600 in the bank, and £136 in the hands of the secretary.

The minutes of that last war-time board meeting contained the following entry:

"Prior to the commencement of the business the Chairman and other Directors referred to the news received this morning that an Armistice had been signed, and the cessation of hostilities as from 11 a.m. This war in which nearly the whole world has been engaged commenced on 29th July, 1914 between Austria and Serbia, and Great Britain entered into it on 4th August, 1914".

It would be impossible to expect that the dry minutes of board meetings could ever convey the sense of upheaval and tragedy that the country, the society and the town of Leek had undergone through those four long years. But the words "nearly the whole world" seem to convey the profound sense of shock that what started out as the short war expected from historical precedent had turned out a war so long in duration — a tragic consequence of the increase in material resources which the 20th century had brought. Those resources had enabled a war to be prolonged for four years. Now they had to be used to win the peace.

The cry was for homes fit for heroes to live in, echoing the ringing tones of Lloyd George's famous speech in Wolverhampton towards the end of the war, asking "What is our task?" and answering "To make Britain a fit country for heroes to live in".

In the years immediately preceding the war, there had been a low level of housing starts. That low level was reduced still further by war. And the existing stock had deteriorated severely from lack of repair and maintenance.

As the war came to its close, The Building Societies Association began to study how it could increase house building and how quickly the devastated building industry could be brought back to health.

The government set up several committees to look at the question of postwar housing policy. One of them, the Salisbury Committee, had as its remit the task of determining how many extra houses would be needed at the war end. It reported in August, 1917, that 300,000 houses would be needed immediately. It proved an estimate that was far too low. By the end of the war the probable shortage was double that amount.

The chairman of The Building Societies Association warned its 1917 conference that building houses for the lower paid worker would require "special solutions". The immediate aftermath of the war was to bring grave disappointment to the hopes of the building society movement, but then was to follow a period of growth and prosperity. The Leek and Moorlands was changed by it into a truly national society as it began to build up a branch and agency network for the first time.

4: On to the National Stage

THE HIGH INTEREST rate policy of wartime government had posed great problems for the building societies. In peacetime, they expected to be asked to play a leading part in the housing programme. But they suffered a severe setback when the government made it clear that local authorities would take the leading role in housing.

But this setback turned to be a very temporary one because of another government policy — the post-war extension of rent control. Its effect was to force many landlords to sell their properties — either to sitting tenants or when the properties fell vacant. In addition, there was rising demand for newly-built houses. Before the war, the building societies were still primarily involved in financing the building of houses to let rather than for owner-occupation. Now the balance was changed as new demand for mortgage finance grew.

Conditions were also right for an inflow of funds to meet this demand. Lower national interest rates, uncertainties in the financial markets and taxation changes all helped to make investment in the societies more attractive.

In the 15 years following the war, more than two million houses were to be built and of these, two-thirds were to be in the private sector.

It was towards the end of 1920 that this investment and building boom began to get up steam in the building society movement. The government cut back on its help to local authorities after nearly 200,000 homes were completed. To protect tenants from the economic effect of the housing shortage in the form of escalating rents, stricter rent controls were enforced.

These controls were even extended to houses with higher rateable value than had been covered in wartime. The result was that the societies came to dominate the housing market but the change was not without problems. After rising steeply in the immediate postwar years, house prices began to fall in 1922 and 1923, although they then began to rise again. In 1921, unemployment rose above the one million mark and stayed above that level for most of the inter-war years. Yet even this lasting obstacle did not dampen the overall demand for housing.

After the small lull of 1922 and 1923, each year proved better and better for the building societies. Mortgage lending and assets increased rapidly. The Leek and Moorlands accounts throughout these years show fully the prosperity building societies were enjoying.

The first post-war report and accounts in 1919 demonstrated how well the society's business had withstood the difficult wartime conditions. They stated that the "striking increases in membership, investors' subscriptions, and advances on mortgages show a considerable improvement in the society's business in the final year of the Great War".

The number of members stood at 6,209 at the 1918 year-end, an increase of 434 over 1917, and the number of accounts at 7,315, an increase of 371. Investors' subscriptions were up by £60,879 to £161,689 and advances were £42,862 up at £70,135.

The lasting resentment among the societies at the financing of the war by high interest rate policies, showed itself at the 1920 annual meeting when Alfred Moore, acting as chairman for the meeting, attacked the government's post-war housing measures in these strong terms:

"If the Government had taken the building societies of the United Kingdom into their confidence during the war, they would not now have had to borrow such a tremendous sum for houses, and members would have owned their own homes".

He referred trenchantly to the interest rates that had been charged by the "moneylenders".

But the directors were still confident of the future. With the expanding trade of Leek, still more homes would be required. The restrictions against increases of rent or obtaining possession of houses were, they felt, "not likely to be continued in their present drastic form".

As the government cut back on its aid to local authority building, and as the private building boom grew, so the Leek's figures reflected the national building society pattern.

The 1921 report described 1920 as "a year of extraordinary progress, all former records being left a long way behind". Assets now were over the million mark for the first time, at £1,039,381. Membership had increased by 785 to 7,812, and accounts by 667 to 8,583.

The society had been compelled to decline a "large amount of business, owing to the receipts, great as they were, being insufficient to meet the abnormal demand for loans".

The Leek and Moorlands now started on its long road to becoming a national society when in January, 1920, its first agency was appointed in Stockport. The first branch office was opened in Biddulph later that year. Further branch offices were opened at Congleton in 1929, and Nottingham in 1930.

In 1924, a presentation was made to Henry Salt to mark his years of chairmanship from 1912. The presentation also marked the completion of an extension to the offices at No. 15 Stockwell Street. A reception was held in the Art Galleries of the Nicholson Institute in the town by the managing director, Arthur Shaw.

Salt, a director and the secretary of Messrs Brough, Nicholson and Hall, one of the major local silk manufacturing firms, received an engraved solid silver plate set, value 100 guineas, which consisted of a "tray, sugar basin, cream jug, tea-pot and hot water jug, and two old Sheffield plate entrée dishes".

The Leek and Moorlands' growing success was in part due to a steady revival in Leek's trade, particularly in the silk industry where the early years of the 1920s were good ones, and wages were reckoned to be very high. Farming was also in a healthy state. The Leek and Moorlands, which had a long tradition of lending to its neighbouring farming community, benefited accordingly.

It was in 1923 that the Leek and Moorlands' growing national importance was marked by a special article in the *Building Societies' Gazette.* The article on July 2nd was one of a series on leading British building societies.

The article began with these words which also referred to the smaller Leek United society:

"Situated amidst beautiful scenery in the North East corner of Staffordshire — ten miles from anywhere — is the old market town of Leek with its 18,000 inhabitants.

"Small though it is, in proportion to its size, Leek is one, if not actually, of the largest towns in England in a Building Society sense, for it possesses two societies whose total assets amount to approximately £2,000,000 . . . . Naturally the little town, and especially the Building Societies, are proud of this astonishing achievement".

The article went into the history of the society and its current business, commenting on the "wonderful progress" that had been made in the past few years.

This exhilarating sense of progress was greatly in evidence at the annual meeting three years later, on March 26th, 1926, at Leek Town Hall, when the chairman of the meeting, Alfred Moore, commented that "The society had certainly grown into a huge concern — a concern such as its founders never contemplated".

A significant feature of the Leek's and of Britannia's business has always been the low management costs, invariably below the average for the movement. This was clearly seen in the 1925 figures presented to the 1926 meeting. The management expenses were, in fact, met entirely by the income on the reserve funds, an unusual situation, even for the Leek.

The Leek was thus in a very strong position to cope with the financial crisis which hit the country from 1929 to 1931. The end of the 1920s showed it developing strongly as a society on modern lines, emphasising lending to owner ocupiers. During the crisis, it met withdrawals promptly, with no loss of interest or bonus for investors.

The National Government, returned with a massive majority at the General Election in October, 1931, brought in a cheap money policy which saw Bank Rate reduced to two per cent by June, 1932, and rates cut on government stock. These measures made building society investment very attractive. Indeed, some months before they were implemented in 1932, the societies had had to place restrictions on incoming funds. Now they were only too willing to follow the call to them by the Chancellor of the Exchequer, Neville Chamberlain, to ease their competitiveness.

Mortgage rates now began to fall to around the five per cent level after staying at around six per cent for a decade. There was no nationally recommended rate at this time and so societies brought in the new rates at different times. The Leek followed in the general move to five per cent. The societies also passed an historical watershed. When there had been rate changes in the past, they had only been on new mortgages. Now for the first time in their history, the societies began to change the rate on existing accounts.

The episode was accompanied by large-scale press publicity. The importance of the building societies in the economic planning of the country was acknowledged for the first time.

These momentous times nationally coincided with a momentous change at the top of the Leek and Moorlands. Four years earlier, on March 26th, 1929, the managing director, Arthur Hugh Shaw, had died, leaving the secretary, Francis Billing, as sole chief executive officer. The long link between the Shaw family and the Leek and Moorlands was finally broken, and tributes were paid not only to Shaw's long record of service but also to the work he had done for The National Association of Building Societies.

Billing himself died, on August 13th, 1933, at the age of 64.

A long illness had afflicted him from the start of the year. He was very much a Leek man through and through, and was deeply involved all his life in the affairs of the town. He was a prominent member of the parish church choir and a leading member of the amateur musical society. At one time, he had been the church choirmaster.

The directors, in their tribute to him, pointed to his contribution in piloting the society to "its present impregnable position".

An obituary in the Building Societies Gazette contained this appreciation: "A man of vision and boundless energy, he had done much to further the progress of the society with which he had been connected for so long".

It was now that the directors took a very farsighted step as they chose a successor to Billing. Hitherto, the Leek had been led and directed entirely by local men. The directors decided to go outside to bring in new leadership to maintain and expand the society's growing role nationally outside of the Staffordshire area. And the man they chose was not yet even in his thirties. They were choosing a leader for many years to come.

Hubert Newton, after attending an interview in Leek for the post of Secretary, started his duties on 1st November, just two months after his 29th birthday on 2nd September. But for so young a leader, he already had wide knowledge of the movement. He was a young man in a hurry, as he himself admits — "in a hurry to gain experience". Since leaving Burnley Grammar School at the age of 14, he had been with four different building societies in different parts of the country — the Burnley Building Society, the Northampton Town and Country Benefit Building Society, the Leeds Permanent Building Society and the Bristol and West of England Building Society.

Newton spent the first five years of his career with his hometown society before moving to the Northampton society (now the Anglia) in 1923 to take the post of mortgage department controller. In 1926, he moved to Leeds as controller of the investment department. While there, he installed the first ever book-keeping machine in a building society office. In 1928, he passed the final examination of the Chartered Institute of Secretaries, and in 1930 was on his way again to become assistant secretary of the Bristol and West of England.

Two men had helped him greatly in this early part of his career. One was Walter Harvey who became general manager of the Burnley during Newton's time there. He became a leading figure in the building society movement, a member of the Council of The National Association of

Building Societies, and a writer on building society issues. His influence on the young Newton was a powerful one.

The other helper was Wiliam Ewart Foulds, who was in part responsible for the many moves of the young Newton. Foulds went from Burnley as secretary to the Northampton society and Newton followed. Foulds then became general manager of the Leeds Permanent and Newton followed. The connection was only broken when Newton went to Bristol.

Newton's ambition as a boy had been to become a professor of mathematics. His father became ill and he had to leave school at 14 to make his way in the world. So great was his capacity for learning that by the time he came to Leek, he was not only a chartered secretary, but also a Fellow of the Royal Economic Society and a Fellow of the Incorporated Society of Auctioneers. He had already carved out a reputation in the movement as a thinker. In September, 1932, he had written a major piece in the Building Societies Gazette on mortgage rates, income tax and building societies, attacking the cheap money calls of the popular press on mortgage rates.

The Leek directors were still local men but they saw in Newton a man who would give them a valuable outside perspective. Newton was quickly to become one of the most influential men in the movement. He was also to become one of the most controversial. A man opposed by instinct to detailed rules and regulations, he was often to be a "maverick" in the movement, consciously and determinedly so. Too many of the so-called agreements imposed on the building society movement he saw as the work of the rich and powerful societies who were determined to safeguard their position at the expense of borrower and investor. But above all, Newton was to turn out to be a fine administrator, enhancing the society's reputation for efficiency at below-average management costs.

He was also to turn himself into a Leek man and still today lives within close distance of the Britannia's headquarters. His involvement with staff, town and community activities was to become legion. He had married his wife, Elsie, just two years before, having met her when she worked for the Leeds Permanent. They stayed at the Red Lion Hotel and Daisy Bank Cottage before moving to a permanent home at Birchall on the outskirts of Leek. His starting salary was £750.

The Building Societies Gazette described his appointment in these words:

"Mr Newton has reached the secretarial chair at a particularly early age but in view of the wide and extensive experience he has gained in the service of important societies in different parts of the country, he will, we feel sure, abundantly justify his selection as the chief executive officer of a society which has been distinguished in the past for the quality of the service it has rendered".

Newton's arrival came just after the building society movement had taken the step of imposing cuts in mortgage rates, in line with Neville Chamberlain's cheap money policy. The previous steady rise in mortgage lending now flattened out although the total of £100 million was reached for the first time in 1933. By that year, the worst was over and the scene set for further progress until the shadows of war loomed once again.

Ironically the depression years stimulated the desire to save. As other financial institutions weakened and other investment opportunities crumbled, so the building societies benefited.

Housebuilding was stimulated by low deposits, longer repayment terms, and low interest rates. Building costs too were falling. In 1931-33, new houses averaged some 210,000 a year, of which private builders accounted for 140,000. From 1934 to 1938, the number averaged 350,000 a year, with private builders contributing about 280,000.

Newton brought in a number of innovations to the Leek and Moorlands' work. In his previous posts, he had played an active role in getting mortgaged property deeds transferred from local solicitors to the head office. He carried out the same change at the Leek. He reorganised the office and general administration and laid down a detailed mortgage lending policy. He also promoted marketing and publicity as important ways of increasing the society's business. To this end, he started the practice of an annual lunch, held in Leek's big urban neighbour, the city of Stoke.

At the first lunch in 1934, Alfred Moore, now president and chairman, pointed out the problems the cheap money policy had brought. Because of the policy, mortgages were being redeemed and it was becoming increasingly difficult for the society to find "suitable mortgage business".

Moore's lament also demonstrated just how national the Leek's business had become. In his words: "We must lend approximately £1 million per annum in order to keep pace with repayments of mortgages and receipts from shareholders. We cannot find this money in Leek. We are obliged to spread our net and your directors have devoted a good deal of time in establishing agencies and offices throughout the country".

"Leek business would keep us employed for about one month in the year, and we rely upon our outside connections to keep us going for the remainder of the year".

Moore died later that year. He was in his mid-80s. Like his predecessor, Henry Salt, he had been a director of the silk firm of Brough, Nicholson and Hall. He had also been president of the Leek Manufacturers and Dyers Association. He was a member of the Leek Urban District council when it was formed in 1894 and was chairman in 1904-06. He was succeeded as the society's president and chairman by another Leek silk industrialist, William Hassall, managing director and secretary of the Leek Silk Twist Manufacturing Society Limited.

Figures issued a year later at the annual meeting on February 25, 1935, in Leek Town Hall, emphasised Moore's point about the society's spread of business, Of 29,947 members, fewer than 2,000 were local. Among 1,040 building societies in the country, the Leek and Moorlands held 20th position in terms of assets.

Besides its branches, the Leek and Moorlands' agencies now covered not only the Potteries area, but towns and cities such as Birmingham, Manchester, Liverpool, Bristol, Preston, Rochdale, Rugby, Buxton, St. Annes-on-Sea, Southport and Market Drayton. In October, 1934, another branch office had been opened — at Ironmarket in Newcastle-under-Lyme.

But the Leek and Moorlands' domestic preoccupations were now to be disturbed by a major split in the building society movement in which it and its secretary, Hubert Newton, were among the leading protagonists.

In 1926, the name of The Building Societies Association had been changed to The National Association of Building Societies. The change marked the growing national character of the association as it came to represent most societies.

Its activities were still mainly those of parliamentary watchdog and public relations body for the industry. It kept away from any interference in the working of individual societies. But by the early 1930s, competition for business was becoming intense and the Association was worried about defaulting buyers as loans were granted generously at a time of falling property prices.

In October, 1931, the Council of the Association felt it necessary to point out to members their responsibilities in lending. A circular stated:

". . . at the executive committee just held, it was felt that societies in union would not take it amiss if a word of caution were given in relation to advances on mortgage. This is that it is felt essential that prospective buyers should have a personal stake in the property to the extent of ten per cent at least of the purchase price, and that, in the interest of the movement, building societies should protect themselves and it by rigid adherence to this practice for the time being".

More guidance was issued shortly afterwards on subjects such as repayment periods and payment of commission.

This growing move towards a code of practice for the industry was strengthened when in 1933, Harold Bellman, chairman of the London-based Abbey Road Building Society, took over the chairmanship of the Association. Bellman campaigned for a Code of Ethics and Procedure which would be binding on the member societies.

The code was put to the Association's members at their conference in Harrogate in 1934. By an overwhelming majority, the conference authorised the Council to submit it to member societies. A two-thirds majority would be needed for approval.

The ready acceptance of the conference was not so apparent when the proposal was circulated nationally. Newton himself had been sceptical about the Bellman campaign for some time. He saw in the proposal an attempt by some societies to safeguard their own positions which had been achieved by some of the methods now being condemned. Abbey Road, along with its London counterpart, the Woolwich Equitable, had been reckoned to be among the fiercest competitors in the market. Both had forged special contacts with builders, estate agents and lawyers in the fight for new mortgage business. By the end of 1933, Abbey Road's total assets were some £41.8 million and the Woolwich's some £23 million.

A revised scheme, aimed at protecting the interests of the smaller societies, was put to members in October, 1934. The proposals were passed overwhelmingly and also at a special general meeting in January, 1935.

But now serious trouble began to arise. Societies had been asked not to make changes in interest rates as these rates might shortly be regulated in the code. But some broke ranks, to which the big London societies responded in turn.

Against this deteriorating background, further revisions were made to the Code in the hope of attracting almost unanimous support. The proposals were put to another vote in February, 1936, and again approved by an overwhelming majority. But 40 societies, representing nearly ten per cent of member society assets, voted against. The Leek and Moorlands was one of them and was the leading voice of dissent. In addition, about 100 of the smaller societies did not vote or expressed doubts.

Could the Leek and Moorlands and it fellow dissenters be forced into acceptance against their will? Fierce disputes broke out over whether acceptance of the Code should be a condition for membership of the Association. The Association tried to solve the problem by calling a special meeting in June, 1936, to dissolve itself and setting up a new Association for which membership was conditional upon acceptance of the Code. The new Association took on the previous name of the National Association, "The Building Societies Association".

Over 200 societies joined but the Leek and Moorlands and over 50 other societies broke away to form a rival organisation, The National Federation of Building Societies. The Leek and Moorlands was the biggest society in the group and Newton's voice the strongest in opposition to the Bellman plans.

The Federation was founded at a meeting at the Friends' Meeting House in London on 7th October, 1936. A council of twelve was set up to administer the new body, among them Hubert Newton who took on the role of conference secretary. National conferences of the Federation, organised by Newton, were subsequently held in London in 1937, Eastbourne in 1938, Torquay in 1939, and London again in 1940.

The president and chairman of the Leek and Moorlands, William Hassall, commented in these terms at the society's annual meeting in February, 1937: "The Building Societies Association set out to introduce a code of ethics. Your directors felt that the code was not sufficiently stringent in its requirements, neither did it give sufficient elasticity without continued reference to a central body. Your directors felt the scheme, designed as it was to check the severe competition — mainly of the larger societies — would be unworkable".

In July, 1938, Newton was elected vice-chairman of the Federation. In May, 1938, at the conference at Eastbourne, he spoke forcefully on the general problems facing the movement and on new trends in lending, commenting that building societies had now got down to the business of "housing the low-paid classes".

But events were now moving to close the split, not least the oncoming threat of war. As Sir Hubert recalls today, the government, with more pressing things on its mind, became irritated at having to deal with two bodies on tax and other issues. And the split had put paid anyway to the idea of a code and detailed regulation.

By 1939, a reconciliation was being sought by both sides. Talks soon led to agreement and the Association and the Federation were merged the following year after their annual meetings had approved the formalities. Newton had now become chairman of the Federation and presided over the final days of the Federation's short existence.

While the Leek had been absent from The Building Societies Association, the Association had brought in an important innovation in 1939 when it began to recommend to societies what rates of interest should be paid on investment income and what rates mortgages should carry. It was a system alien to Newton, who strongly believed that it was up to individual building societies to manage their own affairs and not enter into cartel arrangements. Although he was to rise to lead The Building Societies Association himself, he was to engage in frequent battles against the recommended rates system, earning himself the reputation of the leading "maverick" in the movement. Not until 1983, with the demise of the system, did Newton have the final pleasure of seeing his views win through.

Newton chaired the last annual meeting of the Federation, on 8th May, 1940, at the Piccadilly Hotel in London. The following resolution was passed unanimously:

> Resolved that The National Federation of Building Societies proceed to carry out forthwith the decision to merge with The Building Societies Association taken at the special meeting of members of The National Federation of Building Societies held in London on 20th September, 1939, and that the societies now in union with The National Federation of Building Societies be strongly recommended to join The Building Societies Association, in accordance with its amended rules as approved by the members of The Building Societies Association at their meeting held on 3rd May, 1940.

The episode marked the Leek's most prominent act so far on the national stage of the building society movement.

During this period of upheaval, the Leek and Moorlands took its first step along the merger trail, with the takeover of the Longton Mutual Permanent Benefit Building Society which had its office at Longton, Stoke-on-Trent. The takeover took place in October, 1938. The assets of the Longton were £70,000. This was very small by comparison with the size of the Leek, but the Longton business complemented the Leek very well geographically.

By this time, the society's business was outgrowing its home at 15 Stockwell Street. It was decided to buy the building next door, Stockwell House, demolish it and build a new headquarters building in its place. New Stockwell House was completed in 1937, with a board room on the first floor and cellars and strong rooms in the basement to keep the society's archives, together with all the important legal documents relating to the transactions of members.

The foundation stone was laid on Friday, 19th June, 1936, on a "gloriously sunny day", as it was described at the time. The ceremony was performed by William Hassall. He recalled to his audience that in the old days, the Leek and Moorlands had been a local society, serving the interests of Leek and its moorlands, as its name implied. Now it had become "one of the premier national societies".

A major ceremony marked the completion in 1937, and Sir Enoch Hill, one of the leading figures in the building society movement, was invited to perform the opening on 28th October. Hill had become famous not only as the chief executive of Britain's biggest building society, the Halifax, but also as the chairman of The Building Societies Association and of The National Association of Building Societies, from 1921 to 1933.

It was not just Hill's fame in the movement that made him the ideal guest. He was a Leek man himself, born in humble circumstances in 1865. He started work in the town at the age of eight as a half-timer, earning one shilling a week. Eventually he was to join the Leek United, and to become its secretary. His one connection with the rival Leek and Moorlands was that he bought his house through their mortgage. He left the town to join the old Halifax Permanent society as secretary in 1903 and was instrumental in its merger with the Halifax Equitable in 1928 to create the giant society we know today. He had also stood, while with the Halifax, as Unionist parliamentary candidate for Leek in 1922 and 1923, being defeated both times by his Labour opponent.

So many people gathered to watch the opening that traffic had to be diverted. Hill was handed a gold key to unlock the door of New Stockwell House. A lunch was held afterwards at the North Stafford Hotel, Stoke, when Hill referred to the Leek's Longton merger and asked jokingly whether the Leek would now absorb the Halifax.

The Leek's president and chairman, Hassall, was ill, and so a letter was read out from him instead, paying warm tribute to the advances made under Newton's leadership. "If there had been no Hubert Newton, there would probably have been no New Stockwell House".

Figures were given out at the opening to illustrate this progress. When the society opened its first premises at No. 1 Stockwell Street, in 1856, assets were just £2,800. When it moved to No. 15 Stockwell Street, in 1895, assets were below £500,000. When Newton became secretary in 1933, they had risen to £3,780,000. Now, just four years later, they were £6,000,000.

Francis Billing,
Secretary 1909-1933

Alfred Howard Moore, JP,
President 1932-1934,
Chairman 1927-1934,
Director 1902-1934

The Trustees, Directors, Agents and other Officials on the completion of the extension to the Office of the Society, No. 15 Stockwell Street, Leek, 18th September, 1924.

Seated in the foreground is Sir Arthur Nicholson, JP, CC, President. (Taken on the steps to the Nicholson Institute, Leek). Directors: R. W. Brealey, F. L. Burton, J. Morton, H. E. Salt, F. Carding, A. H. Shaw, W. Hassall, S. M. Phillips, A. H. Moore. Trustee Anthony Ward. Staff: F. Billing (Secretary), H. Ind (Accountant), A. Halton, R. C. Johnson, H. Ball, C. Birch. Agent H. Morris.

Luncheon at the North Stafford Hotel, Stoke-on-Trent, after the Official Opening of New Stockwell House, Leek, by Sir Enoch Hill, 28th October, 1937.

Left to right, back row: W. Warrington (Chairman, Leek UDC), John Wain (Vice-President), Col. A. F. Nicholson (Director), H. Preston (General Manager, Northampton Town & County Building Society), G. E. Watson (Director), F. G. Johnson (Vice-President), A. Garner (Stockport Agent), S. Myott (Vice-President), J. Ward (Vice-President), H. J. Arundel (Director), J. R. Buckley (Staff Surveyor), Hubert Newton (Secretary).

Front row, seated: C. Birch (Director), D. Fergyson (Director), W. Harvey (General Manager, Burnley Building Society), Sir Enoch Hill (Director, Halifax Building Society), Lt.-Col. G. J. Worthington (Director), F. Carding (Director), G. H. Sheldon (Director), S. M. Phillips (Director), W. A. Furmston (Director).

Even with the new building completed, the directors looked forward to further expansion. Ground at the rear was purchased in case extensions were needed. Under Hubert Newton, the society's development of agencies and branches was proceeding apace and the demands on central office resources were increasing accordingly. There were now agencies and branches in some 80 areas throughout the country.

The efficiency with which the society had been run was pointed out at the annual meeting earlier in the year in February. The society had one of the lowest mortgage rates in the country, charging 4.25 per cent to all borrowing members, old and new, while preserving the high interest rate of 3.5 per cent to existing shareholders. And expenses were still going down as a percentage of funds administered.

The records of the following year's annual meeting show how the prospect of another war was exercising minds. A National Defence Contribution scheme had been set in train by the government, and Hassall compared it to income tax which had come in for a war emergency only and had never been rescinded:

"I hope that when the tax expires in 1942, it will be abolished, and that something of the spirit of Christian civilisation will be the true guiding force of all the nations who today are preparing for something which, I hope, can be avoided".

Hassall also drew the meeting's attention to the war risks clause in insurance policies covering mortgaged property:

"During the last few months, large numbers of insured in this country have received intimation with their notices of renewals of fire and householders' comprehensive policies that all the risks of war and of civil war will be excluded from the beginning of this month.

"The necessity for inclusion of this clause is to be regretted, but your Society, through The National Federation of Building Societies, is making strenuous efforts for some legislation to be passed empowering the Government to underwrite this risk".

Hassall did not live to see the war. He died on 18th August, 1938, at the age of 83, having been a director for 31 years. Besides his role as a prominent local industrialist, he had also been an alderman on Staffordshire County Council. His successor as chairman was Lt.-Col. Guy Worthington, a prominent local figure and private school headmaster. His successor as president was Sir Ernest Johnson, a leading pottery manufacturer.

In the year the war broke out, another act was passed of major importance for the building society movement, the Building Societies

Act, 1939. This resulted from a legal case started in the High Court in January, 1938, which became the most famous in the history of the movement.

The case involved the Bradford Third Equitable Benefit Building Society and one of its borrowers, a Mrs Elsie Borders, of 81 Kingsway, Coney Hall, West Wickham, Kent. She had bought her house in Coney Hall, a new residential estate on the edge of the Kent countryside, for £730, on a mortgage of £693. The normal amount should have been 75 per cent only of the price, around £550. But in the 1930s, many building societies, including the Leek, entered into "pooling agreements" with housebuilding firms. The builders provided collateral security so enabling the building society to make larger advances.

Mrs Borders withheld her mortgage payments because of alleged defects in the house although the builders' brochure had said that the house would be thoroughly inspected by the building society inspectors many times during its construction. The contention that shook the building society movement was that the collateral security taken by the building society rendered the mortgage *ultra vires* the Rules of the Society although *intra vires,* The Building Societies Acts. Mrs Borders sought the return of all mortgage payments paid previously and damages for what she claimed was fraudulent misrepresentation.

The case dragged on through the courts until the Lords ruled against Mrs Borders in 1941. But it had from its start attracted so much national interest that the Act was passed in 1939 laying down detailed conditions for building society lending and setting rules so stringent for the "pool" system that it was never seen again after the war years.

Hassall had commented on it in these terms at the 1937 meeting of the society:

"We have been inundated with inquiries from large builders endeavouring to negotiate terms with us, but our reply has been, and will continue to be, that we do not seek, neither shall we accept, unduly competitive business. The security of the investors is our main concern, coupled with a reasonable rate of interest allowed to them, and as low a rate as practicable charged to the borrowers".

The last annual meeting of the Leek and Moorlands, before war broke out, was on 22nd February, 1939. The new chairman echoed the old in hoping for a peace that was not to come:

"I think it can be said that the year 1938 has been the most eventful one for the past 20 years. The European crisis, culminating in the Munich agreement, is one which we are not likely to forget. I do not intend to refer to the political value or otherwise of the agreement, but those whose destinies are wrapped up in the building societies movement are particularly thankful that we have secured peace for the time being, and, I hope, for many years to come".

It was on 31st August, 1939, just before the outbreak of war, that the board faced a major decision on interest rates. Bank Rate had risen suddenly to 6 per cent because of the war crisis, and the cheap money policy was at an end. The mortgage rate was put up to 5.5 per cent on new mortgages, and existing borrowers reverted to the 5 per cent level prior to the cheap money policy.

So the war had had its effect even before it started. Moreover, mortgage business was already severely reduced because of the nationally imposed cutback in building, and the control of materials and labour to prepare for the war effort.

Public confidence in the building society movement nevertheless still remained high. It had been tested already at the time of the Munich crisis by the success of the societies in meeting withdrawals. There was no panic on the outbreak of war, despite severe pressure on funds and the expected heavy withdrawals. But the Second World War was to pose a greater domestic worry to building societies than the First World War because of the far greater war damage at home. Bank Rate was soon cut as the government embarked on low interest rate policies to finance the war, in contrast to the high interest rates of the First World War. This stopped the competition of high coupon government stock but it made it difficult for the societies to secure adequate returns. But the crisis of war was once again to prove how soundly based were the finances of building societies.

5: Out of the Ashes of War

BANK RATE WAS cut back from 6 per cent to 2 per cent in October, 1939, and stayed at this level through the war. It was in taxation where war finance weighed heaviest with the standard rate of income tax rising to 7s. in the £ at first, and then to 8s. 6d. in two budgets in 1940, and lastly to 10s. in 1941 where it stayed. This meant that the composite rate paid by building societies went up in line too — a great burden for them to bear.

The first annual meeting to be held during the Second World War was on 21st February, 1940, at Leek Town Hall as usual. The meeting received the report for 1939 in which the directors described "another successful year" and progress "indicating that the Society continues to enjoy the confidence of its members and of the general public".

The chairman, Lt.-Col. Worthington, referred to his previous remarks at the last peacetime meeting:

"When last I had the pleasure of addressing you, I said in my opening remarks that the year 1938 was probably the most eventful one for 20 years. Well, it is no pleasure to me to say now that its eventfulness has been eclipsed by the year 1939. The outbreak of war, which was so narrowly averted in 1938, was found to be unavoidable in 1939. On 3rd September, it could no longer be delayed in view of Hitler's activities following the Munich Agreement, and became an established fact. This movement of ours is truly democratic and we view with serious concern and sympathetic feelings the outrages committed against small, industrious and democratic peoples. I refer to the invasion, occupation and eventual suppression of the States of Austria, Czechoslovakia and Poland by the adoption of methods which can only be described as medieval in their barbarity".

The 1939 Building Societies Act was now beginning to take effect and was welcomed in these terms by Worthington:

"The new Building Societies Act will, I think, assist the movement in standardising the practice and bringing to the notice of intending borrowers all the facts concerning mortgage advances. I might mention that your own Society has never taken collateral security in respect of advances without bringing such fact to the borrower's notice before the mortgage deed was signed".

Part of the administrative problem facing the Leek and Moorlands was the flood of wartime administrative measures flowing out of Whitehall. Worthington referred to 2,000 acts or orders so far enacted, many of which affected property.

He also pointed out that of the 14,444 mortgages held by the society, only 317 had been affected by wartime conditions, and arrangements had been made with the borrowers for them to make interest payments only. The arrangements would be reviewed every three months.

He added:

"There are 28 exceptions to these arrangements, and these relate to mortgagor members serving with the armed forces, and where the Government has not so far communicated its decision to make additional allowances for which application has been made".

The Leek and Moorlands' business held steady during the first year of war. At the end of 1940, total assets dropped slightly from £6,914,530 at the previous year-end to £6,906,095. This was the first time the society had suffered a fall since the First World War. The directors reported: "during the whole of the year under review the Society has operated under war conditions. Despite this, another successful year has been experienced and the Reserves strengthened to meet further contingencies".

On interest rates, the directors reported that "notwithstanding a substantial increase in the standard rate of Income Tax to 8s. 6d. in the £ involving an additional payment of almost £25,000 in the year 1940", the society paid out a quarter per cent above the average for the movement. But from 1st January, 1941, there would be a cut of a quarter per cent to three per cent for shareholders who had the maximum holding of £5,000.

There was to be no shortage of investment money and the society encountered no trouble in the concessions it made to borrowers who needed to suspend repayment of capital. Indeed in the latter part of the war, it became necessary to restrict investments from members.

The pattern of withdrawals naturally reflected the progress of the war with the heaviest withdrawals coming during the many crises in the opening years. The fall of France in 1940 led to a particularly heavy period of withdrawals for all societies and the government made a Defence Regulation allowing societies to require six months' notice of withdrawal. The Treasury issued an explanatory statement pointing out that the regulation was permissive and that the public should be able to continue to withdraw small sums.

The crucial issue facing the building societies was whether they should meet the extra financial burdens of war by cutting rates to investors or increasing the mortgage rate. The mortgage rate had dropped to 4.5 per cent and the societies felt strongly that it would be against the spirit of the war effort to increase it. So it was investors who took the brunt. By the end of 1942, the share rate had fallen to 2.5 per cent. After that as funds started to flow in, with the tide of war turning, the rate was cut to 2 per cent and even 1.75 per cent for new money, although it was held at 2.5 per cent for existing share accounts.

The low level of activity in the housing market saw mortgage lending fall to a low of £10 million in 1941. It rose to £16 million in 1942, to £28 million in 1943, and £52 million in 1944.

The Leek and Moorlands directors made clear at the start of the war their concern that mortgagors should not suffer. They promised "careful and sympathetic consideration" to all borrowers affected by war.

At the 1941 meeting, Worthington referred to the heavy taxation burden on societies and its effect on their margins:

". . . . the position of our own society was that in a single year, the contribution by way of taxation on practically the like capital structure went up by something like 66.6 per cent, and this is general throughout the movement.

"We have to face also the added burden of the mortgagees' contribution under the War Damage Bill — this being in the nature of the price the building societies will have to pay for the protection of their capital assets, as evidenced by mortgage balances, and this will be a five-year contribution at least. It is clear, therefore, that building societies are facing a narrowing profit margin, and, owing to unsettled conditions, little can be done to increase the earning capacity by new lending".

The Leek and Moorlands ran a series of advertisements during 1941 in the Building Societies Gazette which briefly recounted parts of its own history. The series was entitled "A building society in the making". The society still used its old description of "the largest Staffordshire building society" but one of the advertisements carried a new city flavour. According to the advertisement, the Leek and Moorlands "combines the conservatism and solidity of the country with the modernity of the city".

In 1941, Newton was elected to the Council of The Building Societies Association following the merger of the Association and The National Federation of Building Societies. He was the first

Leek and Moorlands man to be so honoured since the days of Arthur Shaw. He was one of four Federation men to come onto the Council and was to serve on it with distinction for the next 34 years.

During the same year, he was also elected to the Council of The Building Societies Institute, the educational body of the movement, and vice chairman of the Midland Association of Building Societies. He was elected chairman of the Midland Association the following year. On 14th July, 1941, he took on the new title of General Manager to the Leek and Moorlands, retaining the position of Secretary.

From 1940 to 1942, he served as a councillor on the Leek Urban District Council. He took charge of the local platoon of the Home Guard, and carried out fire watching duties. Some 20 members of the society's staff were called to the services. All were to return safely.

In 1942, Newton was appointed a member of The Building Societies Association Reconstruction Committee under the Association's president, Lond Sankey. In 1943, he was invited to join the Emergency Committee of the Association. This was a major accolade for the committee contained just six members. They were effectively the guides and the guardians of the movement during the difficult wartime years.

On 9th November, 1942, the society commemorated its past when it made a presentation to its vice chairman Sidney M. Phillips to mark 70 years of continuous service by the Phillips family to the Leek and Moorlands. His father, Edwin Phillips, had been a director from 1874 to 1921, serving also as vice-chairman. The presentation consisted of a gift of a silver salver engraved with the seal of the society and the signatures of the board.

The Leek and Moorlands lent a brotherly hand of help during these years to the Eastbourne Mutual Building Society, a society very much in the front line of enemy action. It stored the Eastbourne society's title deeds and documents in its own vaults. The kindness was remembered in 1947 when the Eastbourne directors presented a cut-glass water jug, a set of tumblers and an inscribed tray to the Leek and Moorlands chairman.

The episode was to be recalled agan in 1954 when the end of Newton's tenure of office as chairman of The Building Societies Association was marked by a farewell tribute from the manager of the Eastbourne, Gilbert J. Anderson, who recounted Newton and the Leek's generosity:

"During the war, when I was promoted to the rank of manager, 'tip and run' raids were fierce on the Channel coast. I happened to meet Mr

Newton a few weeks after they began, and he asked me how I was getting on. I put a bold face on it, I hope, but he at once put his finger on my real trouble and asked 'what are you doing about your deeds'. I said there was nothing I could do about them; there was no strong room within 80 miles — at least on this side of the Channel — and they were right in the middle of the target area. He did not take two seconds to make up his mind. He said, 'send them to me, I have room, and I will look after them for you'. My directors were never more relieved than when that generous offer was made, and gratefully accepted, and we have never forgotten and never will, that wonderful gesture".

The 1942 report and accounts showed that the War Damage Act was working to the satisfaction of the building societies removing the financial uncertainty over destruction of property. The societies' previous fears about the legislation had subsided. The report stated:

"Under the War Damage Act, 1941 and 1942, the sum of £6,151 has been provided in the Appropriation Account No. 6 for the War Damage Contributions and Premiums which fall to be borne by the Society. The amount, together with the amount of £11,241, provided in 1941, constitutes the total tax liability for the two years, as far as can be ascertained. Future instalments will be provided for in the years in which they become due.

"It has been the constant endeavour of the society to assist borrowers whose mortgaged properties have suffered war damage, by the completion of various forms for submission to the War Damage Commission, by advice on procedure, and by granting temporary loans for repairs until such time as the claim is settled and the loan repaid by the War Damage Commissioners".

By 1943, the tide was turning in the war and the Leek and Moorlands could at last start thinking realistically about its post-war future. At the annual meeting on 17th February, Worthington referred to the 8th Army victory in North Africa, the Russian counter-offensive and the Allies' air superiority in Western Europe. He added: ". . . . we now feel entitled to be considering our plans for the situations which are likely to arise when victory has been won".

Worthington also referred to the effects of enemy bombing on the society's mortgaged properties. There were surprisingly few complete losses considering the Leek and Moorlands' wide geographical spread, even though Leek itself did not suffer heavily.

"You will see details of 49 properties, 48 of which I am sorry to say no longer exist. They were completely demolished as a result of enemy action. Claims for value payments have been lodged with the War

Damage Commission, and you need have no fears but that in due course, payment will be forthcoming from the Government".

The Economist took up the theme of post-war reconstruction in an article in October, 1943, which in many ways anticipated the future peacetime merger policy of the Leek and Moorlands.

The article looked at the role of the building societies in reconstruction and stated that "as to the future of the movement, there are some who advocate a rigid regional grouping of local societies to work co-operatively with planning authorities in their regions. Among a number of objections to the proposal, one stands out: the bulk of building society advance work has long since ceased to be done by local societies.

"Yet there is still room for the grouping of the small local societies whose present separation springs more from sturdy independence than from any economic motive.

"The object is not to produce super-sized building societies — the large societies are probably large enough — but to encourage the growth of moderate-sized units, with keen local interests, stronger finances and more efficient management. This process must be unforced and gradual; it should involve neither aggressive empire building nor the marriage of giants".

After 1942, there was a growing surplus of funds in the movement. By 1944, with the prospect of victory in sight, the surplus was almost embarrassing. There was only a limited amount of mortgage business in which to use the funds, and yet the low rate of return on money invested in government securities, made societies anxious to get as much of the business as they could. Early in 1944, some societies decided on a new aggressive policy: lower mortgage rates, offers of loans for periods up to 30 years, and offers to base mortgages on wartime values which had risen considerably.

This drew upon them the anger of Newton. In 1944, he told the Midland Association of the outcome of the BSA Emergency Committee's discussions on the problem with the district associations:

"We agreed to disagree on domestic matters concerning rates of interest to shareholders and borrowers, payment of commission to agents, solicitors and others and the basis of lending, having regard to wartime values . . . . We have had occasion during the past twelve months to frown on the actions of certain societies in this country and to view with grim concern the wide publicity given to their manoeuvres". The situation was not to abate until the post-war years.

In July, 1944, one of the Leek and Moorlands staff who joined the armed services, Norman Bishop, was promoted to the rank of squadron leader in the RAF. He was 27 and had enlisted in 1939. Since March, 1942, he had been serving in India. His elder brother, Kenneth, had been a member of the Leek and Moorlands staff from 1927 to 1937 before leaving to join the Hanley Economic Building Society, where he was appointed Secretary just four months before joining the forces.

Tragically, Kenneth was killed in a flying accident on 4th August, 1940. By 1945, victory was clearly inevitable. Worthington reported to the annual meeting of the Leek and Moorlands on 21st February: "The War Damage Act has been a blessing to most property owners, and, although difficulties have arisen and will arise over the interpretation of the Act itself, our experience with the War Damage Commissioner is most satisfactory. The Commissioner and his staff are to be congratulated on doing a most difficult job in a most fair and helpful manner".

The Leek and Moorlands' annual contribution to the war damage fund stood then at £8,500. After the slight fall in assets at the start of the war, the society had seen a steady increase although it had to restrict incoming investment money as part of the general wartime restrictions. Worthington pointed out the tremendous competition for mortgage business as the war neared its end:

"Competition for any available mortgage is more severe today than at any time in the history of the building society movement. The high degree of liquidity which is general now in the building society movement, and indeed among lenders generally, coupled with the low rates of interest on Government securities, is forcing a position where a reduction of rates of interest on mortgages may be the next step towards forcing up the growing tempo of competition. Your own society has taken the 'bull by the horns' and reduced the rate of interest on all satisfactory house and farm mortgages".

This was Worthington's last address as chairman although he was to remain a member of the board until 1970. He stepped down in April in favour of Gilbert Tatton, a local industrialist. Tatton was a director of Sir Thomas and Arthur Wardle, a major dyeing company in Leek. He was also a member of Leek Urban District Council and chairman of its gas and electricity committee.

The success of societies in coping with the many financial problems of war was to be sharply jolted as the war came to its close. The new Labour Government under Clement Attlee made it clear that the thrust of the post-war housing plan would be through the local authorities. Strict cost ceilings were imposed on private housebuilding and sales in excess of the purchase price were ruled out for a succeeding period of four years. To rub salt into the wounds, funds were made available for local authorities to buy owner-occupied houses for letting.

Of the one million homes built under the Attlee Government, only 180,000 came from the private sector. Some members of the Attlee Government made no secret of their hostility to building societies. The Minister of Health, Aneurin Bevan, who had responsibility for housing, made a long-remembered attack on the societies as "voracious money lenders", supporting speculative housebuilders and encouraging people to take on mortgages that would turn into "gravestones *(sic)* around their necks".

Nevertheless, building society business soon began to grow fast, although for several years this was largely a process of overhauling the backlog of business held up by the war. The societies were also helped by their financing sales from the private rented sector.

At the annual meeting on 27th February, 1946, at Leek Town Hall, the President of the society, Sir Ernest Johnson, described the peacetime situation. Johnson had missed many of the wartime meetings because of trade work for the government, which had frequently taken him on missions abroad. He now used the occasion to make a strong attack on Bevan:

"Mr Bevan's latest housing subsidy plans may lead to the building of a few more houses, but they show a complete lack of grasp of the essentials of the problems and of their real financial effect".

". . . . Unfortunately, Mr Bevan will have nothing to do with the alternative which private enterprise can offer the country now. The building industry is only too anxious to get on with the business of building houses while I understand that the building society movement as a whole can guarantee to make available as much as £150,000,000 a year for the next ten years to finance house purchase".

In his speech, Sir Ernest pointed out that there had been practically no housebuilding since the start of the war. Yet the increased number of families had boosted demand:

"Whilst there is every reason why houses to let should be first priority it is not every member of the community needing a house who wants a corporation or council rented one. One hopes that the Government and local authorities will see that the needs of the community as a whole, and not one section only, will be dealt with on a fair and equitable basis. The future demand is immense. The task of fulfilling it can be eased by the willing co-operation of all whose business has been, and still is, to assist in the provision of houses. In the fulfillment of that task the building societies will respond to the requirement asked of them and your own Society will be in the forefront with financial assistance on the lowest practicable terms".

The figures for the last year of the war showed how well the society's fortunes had withstood the strains. Assets had increased by £661,000 during the year to stand at £8,726,210 at the year-end. The new business figure for mortgages was a record at £1,892,480 and so was the new mortgages figure at 2,293. Management expenses still remained well below the average for the movement They were at the same percentage level as the pre-war period in spite of the increased costs of labour, postage, printing and standing charges.

The first full year of peace brought further prosperity to the society. The asset figure at the end of 1946 rose to over £11 million. Mortgage advances were double the figure for 1945 at £3,800,000.

This advance in mortgage business in spite of the government's concentration on council house building, came about partly because rented houses were being turned over to sitting tenants in large numbers. There were some six million pre-1919 houses in the country and many had been subject to continuous rent control since 1915. In addition, there were 500,000 houses built in the 1930s for rent and not subject to rent control. Many were bought by speculators who specialised in selling them off to tenants.

The freezing of ownership during the war of many already owner-occupied houses led to a high turnover after the war because of the delayed effect of population movement. This too meant heavy business in fresh mortgage advances.

At the end of 1945, the national total of mortgage lending had risen to £97 million. It rose to £188 millon in 1946, £240 million in 1947, and averaged £270 million a year from 1948 to 1951. The record inter-war figure was £140 million in 1936. Although they were not financing many new houses, most building societies were clearly doing good business. The rate on existing mortgages had been reduced to 4.5 per cent through the war, although new wartime mortgages carried a 5 per cent rate. The rate fell to 4 per cent in 1945 and it remained there throughout the tight interest rate policy of the Labour Government — up until 1952 when the general level of interest rates began to rise again. Until 1950, most societies had to maintain restrictions on the intake of money.

In August, 1946, came a proposal for what would have been the Leek and Moorlands' first post-war takeover. It involved the neighbouring Hanley Economic Building Society, and the terms were recommended to the members of both societies. The plan came to grief at a special meeting of the Hanley society on 19th November, 1946. The resolution approving the amalgamation failed to attain the three-fourths majority legally necessary.

The failure led to some bitter comment from the Leek and Moorlands chairman, Gilbert Tatton, at the following annual meeting in February, 1947. He said the merger would have served the society well as there was "substantial business" to be obtained by amalgamation with "some well-known society in that area." He added:

"The legal procedure to give effect to the views of the two boards is somewhat complicated; but not only is it complicated, but I venture to say it is almost farcical. Although the vast majority of Hanley members (over 3,000 of them) expressed their written approval of the terms of the amalgamation, yet at the special meeting convened to submit the motion, such motion was carried by a bare majority only, whereas the law requires a three-fourths majority. The net result at that meeting was that just under 300 members, who voted against the merger, settled the fate of the society, even though over 3,000 members had assented in writing to the amalgamation. The minority ruled and the amalgamation did not proceed."

These post-war years saw the Leek and Moorlands gradually rebuild its normal pattern of life in the local community. In 1947, the chairman was able to report that all members of the staff who had served in the forces had now returned safely home. On Friday, 23rd April, 1948, the first staff dance since the war was held. The venue was the Town Hall, Leek, and "some 150 dancers" were recorded as being present. Mr and Mrs Newton presented prizes for the winners of the speciality dances. The first annual luncheon at Stoke for ten years was held on 30th September. Earlier, in June, the head office staff had gone on a day trip to Manchester, followed by dinner at the Café Royal and a visit to the Palace Theatre to see "Follow the Girls."

Newton resumed in earnest his deep peacetime involvement in the local community. One of his chief interests was the Rotary movement. He had been the founder president of the Leek Rotary Club in 1937. His post-war activity was not confined to the Potteries area but spread farther afield as he gave a series of talks on building societies which took him to towns such as Sandbach, Ilkeston and even Middlesbrough. He was also prominent in local masonry, eventually becoming master of the Crusader's Lodge of Stoke-on-Trent. He also opened church sales and other events and took part in local golf and tennis tournaments. In this hectic pace of business and social life, he was greatly helped by his wife. "Pip" and Elsie became jocularly known as the King and Queen of

Leek. The nickname "Pip" had been with Newton since his schooldays. It was a pun on Sir Isaac Newton's experiments with gravity. The Pippin apple variety was mentioned during a physics lesson and the tag "Pip" duly applied. It was to be Newton's nickname throughout the wider building society movement.

In June, 1947, he was appointed to the board of the Leek and Moorlands, a move acknowledged in the *Building Societies Gazette* in the following terms: "The latest act of recognition by his directors of his splendid record of service will be extremely popular in building society circles." He had previously served as an ex-officio member. In July, 1948, he was elected vice-chairman of the Stoke-on-Trent branch of the Chartered Institute of Secretaries.

A long-awaited staff pension scheme was finally set up on 1st April, 1947. The matter had first been brought before the board as far back as 1934.

On 13th September, 1948, silver salvers enscribed with the board's signatures and the seal of the society were presented to Lt.-Col. Worthington and Mr Dennis Fergyson to mark their 20 years' membership of the board.

Newton himself remained bitterly critical of Aneurin Bevan and his housing policies in these immediate post-war years. In his speech to the first post-war luncheon at Stoke in 1948, Newton attacked the policy of widespread building of prefabs. Bevan, he said, preferred that the country should continue to pay £1,600 to £2,000 each for "prefabricated monstrosities now littering the countryside." In his view, the private builder "freed from many of the restrictive controls under which he laboured" would have produced a far better house at less cost. Later a double annual lunch was introduced with the Russell Hotel, London, being chosen as the second venue. The Stoke lunches were held in May and the London lunches in November.

Even at the very end of the post-war Labour Government, Newton did not relent in his hostility. In 1951, he was appointed deputy chairman of The Building Societies Association and embarked on a national round of duties. He proposed the toast at a luncheon in Wednesbury on 19th September, 1951, to mark the centenary of the Wednesbury Building Society. The following month the Conservatives were to return to power in the General Election. He told his audience that this meeting was an occasion when the people of the country "might be reminded that the spirit of voluntary thrift still was the greatest quality which any nation could possess."

He continued: "What sort of people are we being driven to become?

Looking back over the past 100 years, and reviewing what has been achieved by voluntary thrift, there is nothing I can see for which representatives of voluntary thrift organisations need reproach themselves; nor can it be said that savings could have been achieved at less expense, with more economy, with more efficiency, than they have been through the medium of organisations like building societies and friendly societies.

"So today I venture to suggest that those who save money in building societies, those who purchase their houses through building societies — representing as they do, over four million of the population of this country — are entitled to receive, from any Government, encouragement, assistance, to continue unhampered the great work which they have been doing for so long."

On Bevan, now departed from the government, he made the following comment: "We have been told by a politician, a man who at one time occupied Cabinet rank, that we are moneylenders. What of the trade unions who have millions of pounds of surplus funds today, are they not moneylenders? Is not the Government, which finances local authorities with funds supplied by the public, a moneylender?"

The town's Labour MP, Mr Stanley Evans, replying to the toast of "The Borough of Wednesbury," remarked that for a centenary party, it was proving to be a pretty lively occasion. He thought that "Sugar Ray" Newton was in very good form. But, of course, this was a non-political occasion.

Earlier in the year at the Leek and Moorlands annual meeting on 26th February, a nostalgic event in the society's own history took place. Mr John Wardle, at 90 years of age still a practising solicitor and partner in the society's head office solicitors firm of Challinors and Shaw of Leek, proposed the vote of thanks to the president, vice-presidents, general manager and staff. He had been a member of the society for 78 years. The *Evening Sentinel* of Stoke reported him as having "spoken with a vigour, grasp of affairs and an aptness that would have done credit to a man half his age." He was to live until 1959.

The annual meeting was able to look back on continued success. A total of £5,068,000 had been advanced in 1950 in mortgages — the highest ever. Assets had increased by £2,314,047 to another record — £19,558,113. These immediate post-war years had been a steady but unexciting time for the building society movement. But they were about to enter a new and very different era, and no society was to change more than the Leek and Moorlands.

6: The Merger Policy Begins

IN THE AUTUMN of 1950, the Conservatives decided on their trump card to oust Labour from power. The party conference pledged the party to build 300,000 houses a year if it were returned to power. The promise was one of the key factors in the 1951 Conservative election success and the task was entrusted by the Prime Minister, Winston Churchill, to Harold Macmillan, the new Minister for Housing and Local Government.

It was not just that the number would be a great increase on the totals achieved by the Attlee Government. The mix of housing would be greatly different for the Conservatives planned to relax the controls on private building.

Surprisingly, the building society movement found itself disappointed by the first two years of Conservative policy. Controls on private building, land development and rents were progressively relaxed but the societies actually saw their total of advances fall marginally in 1952 from the 1951 figure. Newton, who became chairman of The Building Societies Association in 1952 for a two-year term, commented: "The general situation has improved so little that we have some cause for impatience."

But the Macmillan target was achieved in 1953. A total of 318,000 houses were built, although only 63,000 were for owner-occupation.

In 1954, Macmillan gave his first direct fillip to owner-occupation when the government entered into a mortgage guarantee-agreement with the building societies. The agreement brought in guarantees for 95 per cent advances on houses valued at up to £2,000 and built after 1918, and for 90 per cent advances on houses valued at up to £2,500 and built either before or after 1918. The following year, the terms were revised to give a common limit of £2,500 on house values and guarantees for advances up to 95 per cent on houses built after 1918, and 90 per cent on houses built before.

Newton's election as chairman of The Building Societies Association was a mark of honour for him personally and for the Leek and Moorlands' position in the movement. His two years as chairman

No. 15 Stockwell Street, Leek, the former Head Office of the Leek & Moorlands Building Society when it was leased to the Royal Insurance Co. (1938).

The Opening of the Westbourne Chief Office in 1931

Hubert Newton, Chairman of The Building Societies Association, at Church House, Westminster, with HRH Queen Elizabeth The Queen Mother, at an exhibition on the building society movement, past and present. The exhibition and the annual BSA conference were opened by The Queen Mother in May 1954.

Transfer of Engagements. North Staffs Permanent Economic Benefit Building Society to Leek & Moorlands Building Society, 1955. Left to right: A. C. Harvey (N. Staffs), J. W. Lovatt (N. Staffs), Sir Bernard White (Leek), J. W. Shirley (N. Staffs), S. Myott (Leek), Sir Ernest Johnson (Leek), F. L. Davenport (Leek), G. Tatton (Leek).

brought him widespread international contacts. He made several visits to Western Europe, studying housing finance there and consulting with leaders of sister movements. In the autumn of 1953, he made an extensive tour of the United States and addressed several important conferences of executives representing the American equivalents of British building societies. All this was on top of a hectic schedule of activity within Britain, with frequent social and public engagements. Newton also used his term of office to promote closer contact and co-operation with the government over housing affairs.

His first year of office brought this appreciation from the *Building Societies Gazette:* "The serious, uncompromising devotion with which, as chairman, Mr Newton bears the weighty responsibilities of his office in no way precludes the free play of his agile mind and vivacious spirits. These have a way of escaping like the crackle of summer lightning — when the heavens are clear or under the most sombre of skies. Mr Newton has a gay riposte for the most capricious interventions of fate and is able to produce the *mot juste* for every emergency. He is, in short, the ideal compere at life's comedy. As the chairman of any meeting, grave or gay, he is a true gift from heaven, for his happy asides guarantee the good humour that makes for the ready co-operation with the chair that gets business done."

The Leek and Moorlands now began to feel the benefit of the new housing climate. The 97th annual meeting on 22nd February, 1954, at Leek Town Hall heard the chairman, Councillor Gilbert Tatton, point out that all sides of the business had contributed to a year of "excellent progress." Assets were now over £25 million. Shareholders and depositors totalled more than 34,000 and borrowers nearly 24,000.

The President, Sir Ernest Johnson, recalled that he had held the position for 15 years, during which period the savings of members had increased by £16.5 million. He paid tribute to Hubert Newton for this progress:

"In Mr Newton, you have a manager and a secretary second to none in the movement. He is supported by a loyal staff and by excellent agents, solicitors and surveyors throughout the length and breadth of the land."

In 1954, the Leek and Moorlands was given a Grant of Permission to carry arms. The final design was decided on after long and intensive consultation. Its details reflected the long association of the society with Leek and the surrounding moorlands. The shield bore gold masonry with two black flaunches, each charged with a curlew, the bird of the moorlands. The Crest consisted of a gold Stafford knot entwined with flowering sprigs of thrift. The society's motto was included — *"Per frugalitatem domus"* or "Through thrift a home".

Newton's term of office as chairman of The Building Societies Association expired in May, 1954. It was in that month that the Association held an exhibition of the movement, past and present, to coincide with its annual conference held in the Church House, Westminster.

Both the exhibition and the conference were opened by Queen Elizabeth the Queen Mother. Probably never before had the movement been covered so extensively in the national media of the country with both the newspapers and the BBC news programmes reporting the event prominently.

Newton's organisational skills were put to their fullest test and numerous tributes were paid to him at the conference, both on the exhibition and his successful tenure as chairman. The conference ended with all those present spontaneously standing up to give him a personal ovation. The *Building Societies' Gazette* reported on "the all-round virtuosity of his chairmanship."

Newton's talents were soon to be displayed in a different way as he foresaw that the building society movement of the late 1950s and the 1960s would inevitably be more concentrated in its numbers as investors and borrowers became more demanding in the services they expected. In the late 1950s, he began the drive to merger, making the Leek and Moorlands the home for many smaller societies who wanted to come into its fold and benefit from its wider range of services. The policy was to be pursued with energy and determination, and Newton made use of the many contacts he had gained during a lifetime in the movement, to promote it.

In January, 1956, he completed a takeover that consolidated the Leek and Moorlands' already strong position in the Potteries. The North Staffordshire Permanent Economic Benefit Building Society of Newcastle-under-Lyme was merged into the Leek and Moorlands, bringing in assets of over £3 million. This brought the total assets of the Leek and Moorlands to over £34.5 million. The North Staffordshire was a well-established society, dating from 1864.

By the start of 1956, the centenary year of the Leek and Moorlands, the building society movement was beginning to feel the chill wind of the other side of the economic changes brought in by the Conservatives. Part of the Conservative policy was to promote a much more active use of interest rates to guide the economy. The Chancellor, Mr R. A. Butler, had, soon after taking office, raised the then Bank Rate to 2.5

per cent from the 2 per cent level it had stood at for 20 years with one short break. The Bank Rate set the level of interest rates throughout the economy. At first the rise looked a token gesture, but then the rate was raised to 4 per cent, forcing The Building Societies Association to recommend societies to increase their share rate to 2.5 per cent and the mortgage rate to 4.5 per cent. This led to the first significant post-war ripple of dissent in the movement with the Halifax for a time keeping its rates below those of other Association members.

This dearer money policy did not immediately affect the increasing prosperity of the societies and it was not until 1955 that it provided the first serious sign of concern. Bank Rate after two small cuts in 1953 and 1954, jumped at the start of the year from three to four per cent. Later that year, the interest rate on loans made by local authorities for house purchase was raised by 0.5 per cent. Withdrawals from the societies increased heavily while receipts fell.

In July, The Building Societies Association decided to recommend an increase in the share rate to not more than three per cent and to increase the mortgage rate to a minimum of five per cent. This rectified the situation but 1955 marked the first time since the war that building societies had had to face this sort of setback. Investors were becoming interest-rate conscious.

But worse was to come in 1956 and 1957 when a deteriorating economic situation saw Bank Rate shoot up to six and then seven per cent. The nature of the competition was becoming steadily apparent too. Local authorities were giving loans at rates which particularly favoured those paying little or no tax. The hire purchase companies were offering attractive rates and backing their appeal by heavy advertising. And Mr Macmillan, by then the Chancellor, brought in his famous premium bond scheme.

The post-war unity of the movement was now threatened by a new disarray. Newton, unmellowed by his period as leader of the movement, followed his long-held belief that building societies were first and foremost a business and not an arm of government or cartels. They had to respond to market forces like any other business. In May, 1956, the Leek and Moorlands decided that its mortgage rate had to rise to combat the steady deterioration of margins. The uncertainty among societies could not go on. The society broke ranks and increased its mortgage rate to 5.75 per cent for owner-occupiers and six per cent for others. The uncertainty over rates was resolved a few weeks later with The Building Societies Association recommending a share rate of 3.5 per cent and a rate of six per cent on new mortgages. The Leek and

Moorlands brought in the new agreed rates on 1st August.

The centenary year of the Leek and Moorlands was thus a lively one. The annual meeting in the centenary year took place on 27th February at Leek Town Hall when the directors agreed to donate £500 towards the repair of the roof of the Parish Church in Leek. But the month was marred by the death of Mr John Ward, JP, who had been a Vice-President from 1926 to 1955.

The full centenary celebration was in May when a special luncheon was held at the North Stafford Hotel, Stoke-on-Trent. The Duke of Devonshire, President of The Building Societies Association, attended as did the BSA's chairman, Fred Bentley, who was presented as a token with an "enormous" cup and saucer.

The 100th annual meeting took place the following year — on 25th February, 1957. Another death of one of the society's stalwarts was reported — that of the Deputy Chairman, Mr F. Leslie Davenport, JP, who had been a director since 1936. A special meeting of the board the previous month had appointed Sir Bernard White, KBE, to take his place. Sir Bernard, a barrister by training, had been Chief Registrar of Friendly Societies from 1947 to 1954, and so brought a wealth of experience into the Leek. It was also a significant appointment in that Sir Bernard came from outside Staffordshire — his home was in Rye, Sussex. Befitting a national society, the Leek and Moorlands was casting its net for board members farther afield.

Two mergers took place during the year. The Stone New Freehold Benefit Society, based at Stone in Staffordshire, was taken over on 1st August, and the Newcastle-under-Lyme Benefit Building Society absorbed on 31st December. Both were very small but very long-standing local societies. The Stone New Freehold Society had been in operation since 1864, but its assets at the end of 1956 had been just £15,000. The Newcastle-under-Lyme Benefit Society was actually older than the Leek and Moorlands, having started life in 1850. Its assets at the time of the transfer were £153,000.

Towards the end of the year, the Leek and Moorlands found itself engaged in another confrontation with The Building Societies Association, a confrontation much more intense than that of the previous year.

Bank Rate had gone up to seven per cent in September, and in December, the Leek and Moorlands increased its rate on existing mortgages and owner-occupier new mortgages to six per cent. On new mortgages on other types of property, the rate was 6.5 or seven per cent. What led to the move and what irritated the Leek and Moorlands was that through the difficult year of 1957, a small but significant number of the smaller building societies had offered rates of interest for savers above the recommended rate approved by The Building Societies Association, breaking the undertaking they had given to the Association. So in December, the Leek and Moorlands gave notice to the Association of its intention to withdraw from the interest rates undertaking from 31st March, 1958.

Nothing happened up to March to persuade or deter the Leek and Moorlands and it duly carried out its threat. It was followed by a number of other societies in the Midlands. A special appeal was then made to the Leek and Moorlands by the Council of The Building Societies Association, asking it to come back on condition the interest rates undertaking was strengthened. The Leek and Moorlands accepted and, with its Midland compatriots, returned to the fold. The general interest rates situation was eased on 14th August, 1958, when Bank Rate fell to 4.5 per cent. This was the sixth change in the rate since February, 1956. By the end of the year, it had again been reduced — to four per cent.

The merger policy now began to develop apace. Yet another Staffordshire society came into the Leek at the end of 1958, when the members of the Newcastle and District Building Society agreed to transfer their society's business.

This Staffordshire society was founded in 1849, and its assets at 31st December, 1958, were £340,000.

A few months later, the Leek and Moorlands made its most farflung move yet when it took over the Brighton society, the Southdown Permanent Building Society. The transfer took place on 30th April, 1959, and three of the Southdown directors were made local board directors for Brighton and Sussex. Unlike its Staffordshire counterparts, the Southdown was a young society, dating only from 1932. Its assets at the end of 1958 were £307,000. It was not in fact the first southern takeover the Leek and Moorlands had attempted. It followed hard on the heels of an unsuccessful bid for the Sheerness and Gillingham Building Society in Kent.

At the annual meeting of 1959, the Leek and Moorlands chairman, Gilbert Tatton, had made the merger policy clear when he stated that as and when opportunity presented itself, the directors would seek to expand the society's services by acquisition.

A statement on the takeover of the Southdown reiterated that policy. It said that if any smaller society felt its members might be better served by joining forces with a larger progressive society, the Leek and Moorlands "would be willing to consider carefully and sympathetically any proposals regarding a possible merger".

The Leek and Moorlands' attention now turned to Yorkshire, and on 1st October, 1959, the Silsden Building Society of Silsden in the West Riding was absorbed. Its assets at the end of 1958 had been £548,000. It dated back to 1871. The takeovers were also accompanied by expansion of the branch office network. During 1958, offices were opened in Bradford and Macclesfield, and offices in Bristol, Edinburgh and Stockport were opened in 1959.

New Stockwell House was now showing signs of strain following the expansion. An extension was completed in 1959 at the rear of the old premises at No. 15 Stockwell Street, to house the growing files. At New Stockwell House itself, two houses were built at the rear to cater for extra staff.

In October, another important honour fell to Hubert Newton. He was appointed Deputy President of the International Union of Building Societies and Savings and Loans Associations at their International Congress in Johannesburg, South Africa. He succeeded Mr Gordon Collins of South Africa who was appointed President. The union embraced 24 countries where building societies or similar financial institutions operated. The union, first started in 1914, had been reborn after the Second World War, in 1956. Newton had been one of the leading lights in that rebirth, following the international tours he made as chairman of The Building Societies Association.

A reminder closer to home of the Leek's local links came in December when it agreed to support a fund celebrating the 50-year jubilee of the Leek Boys' High School. A sum of 100 guineas was donated.

1959 also saw an important initiative on the national housing front, when the government brought in legislation to encourage the transfer of older houses from landlords to owner-occupiers. The legislation was enshrined in The House Purchase and Housing Act 1959. The general demand for mortgages was high at the time, and with the increase in housebuilding over the 1950s, the societies had tended to concentrate their lending on newer properties. Those who wished to own pre-1919 houses generally had to settle for lower advances and shorter repayment periods. Under the legislation, the government made funds available for the building societies to advance on pre-1919 houses. Advances were to be 95 per cent with the excess advance over 75 per cent being covered by an insurance guarantee policy.

The scheme was to apply to houses of an estimated value of £2,500 with the figure going up to £3,000 in the London area. Societies could take up loans from the Government each month to reimburse themselves. These loans were repayable by half-year instalments over 20 years, at a rate of interest one half per cent less than that charged to the borrowers.

The Leek and Moorlands was a strong supporter of the scheme and was incorporated in it under a certificate dated 16th June, 1959, from the Chief Registrar of Friendly Societies.

The society enjoyed trustee status under section 1 of the Act. By the year-end, it had loaned a sum of £461,000 to 429 borrowers on pre-1919 houses.

Building society rates were now dropping to reflect the plentiful funds coming in. The recommended rate of interest charged on new mortgages on owner-occupied properties fell from six to 5.5 per cent from 1st July. Existing borrowers were given a reduction to 5.5 per cent from 1st October.

The 1950s had been good years both for housebuilding and the funds of the building societies. House prices held steady with a total increase over the decade of just ten per cent. But average earnings doubled and this, combined with the raising of rents on tenanted property, encouraged many families to take on the responsibility of home ownership. By the end of the decade, the proportion of houses in home ownership was 42 per cent. Mortgage advances which had been steady at around £267 million from 1948 to 1952, reached £374 million by 1957 and £560 million by 1960. The number of borrowers increased from 1.5 million in 1950 to 2.35 million in 1960.

The Leek and Moorlands had more than shared in this success. By 1960, it had jumped to a place in the top ten of building societies with assets of £63,329,000.

But for the building society movement as a whole, history was to repeat itself at the end of the decade. The expansion of the late Victorian period had shown up defects in the structure of the movement and led to two major pieces of legislation. Similarly, the good years of the 1950s led to several smaller societies overreaching themselves in their ambition. Regardless of all the previous legislation, it was still possible in the 1950s for four people of no experience whatsoever to fill up a form, pay £10, send rules to the Registrar and begin to invite investments from the public.

During the 1950s, the Registrar had made orders against several small societies, stopping them from inviting subscriptions for shares or money on deposit. In 1958, came a major collapse, that of the Scottish Amicable Building Society. It however, was an eminently respectable society and its error was to have made large investments in undated and long-dated gilt-edged stock. As interest rates rose, so the stock slumped in value. The society had assets of over £25 million and was taken over by the Co-operative Permanent Society. Newton was on very friendly terms with the management of the Scottish Amicable and it is no secret that he would have liked the Leek and Moorlands to have taken on the society. But its financial position was such at that stage that it was simply too big a fish for the Leek and Moorlands to swallow.

The collapse was an unfortunate one but it did not shake the movement as a whole. It was the collapse in 1959 of the State Building Society which was far more serious in its implications, and demonstrated the dangers of small societies expanding too fast.

At the end of 1952, the State Building Society's assets had been just £560,000. By September, 1959, they were over £15 million, accumulated by the society offering very high rates of interest. Half the funds were tied-up in loans to associated property companies. A large amount of the loan cash went to financing speculative takeover bids contrary to the rules of the society and the Building Societies Acts. Disaster struck when one of the bids went wrong. Funds of £3.25 million were lent with no resulting security while a financial wrangle took place over entitlement to shares and cash.

Two of the State Building Society's executives were jailed, and the Chief Registrar secured the appointment of a new board of directors. Mr J. H. Robertson, a former general manager of the Abbey National, was brought in as manager. The society was later absorbed into the Abbey National but the immediate result of this collapse was new legislation in the form of the Building Societies Act, 1960.

7: Goodbye to the Moorlands

SO FAR THE takeovers of the Leek and Moorlands had been of small societies. Now the takeovers were to grow rapidly both in number and in the size of the societies absorbed. The 1960s and 1970s were to see the Leek more active in the merger field than any other building society in the country.

The decade began not only with what was one of the biggest takeovers yet in the history of building societies but also the most unusual of all the Leek's takeovers before and since. For on 1st July, 1960, the Leek and Moorlands took over the internal building society of one of Britain's biggest unions, the National and Local Government Officers Association. The takeover catapulted the Leek into eighth position in the building societies movement in assets.

Curiously it was the innocuous-sounding House Purchase and Housing Act, 1959, which led to the merger. Its requirements for trustee status caused a number of problems for some quite reputable building societies. The NALGO Building Society was one. It found it could not take on "trustee status".

At that time, its assets were £13,146,592. It had been founded in 1932 when NALGO was exclusively a union for local government officers. Indeed, many would have railed at the title "union". It was proud of the name "association" and in fact, was not to register with the Trades Union Congress until 1964. It remains to this day the biggest union not affiliated to the Labour Party.

In 1932, it had 61,000 members and, for some years, its provident fund had been lending its surplus funds in mortgages to help members buy their own homes. In that year, the total advanced reached £36,000 and demand threatened to outrun the cash available. So the union decided to follow through the logic of some of its members lending to other members, and set up its own building society.

In 1936, the NALGO President Billy Lloyd was able to claim that no building society had ever done so well in so short a space of time. In three and a half years, it had lent £2 million at the lowest interest rate in the country — 4.25 per cent — and was paying four per cent tax-free to 14,000 investors.

After the war, NALGO expanded beyond its local government confines to take in managers in the new public industries of gas, electricity, and water, and also into the new National Health Service and municipal transport undertakings. But this expansion was not enough to draw in the amounts of money required to finance increasing mortgage demand from members and the society began to appeal for funds from outside the union's membership. Occasionally, the society was forced to pay a higher rate than other societies, yet it continued to maintain a lower mortgage rate. The result was that lack of investment income forced it to ration the number and amount of its mortgages.

The NALGO Building Society ran into problems over the 1959 House Purchase and Housing Act because the terms of the Act denied trustee status to societies with minimum reserves less than two per cent of total assets. Lack of this status meant that trustee funds could not be invested in such societies. Because of the drop in the value of gilt-edged securities at this time, the NALGO Building Society reserves had fallen well below this level. Trustee investments were therefore denied it, and so it lost any chance of attracting enough funds to meet the ever-growing demands of members for mortgage funds.

For a time, it looked as if the NALGO society would have to be wound up, and this would have caused an immense amount of hardship and difficulty to its members who had invested their money in it and to those who were buying their homes through it.

The manager of the society, George Lees, a former Woolwich Equitable man, saw that a solution lay in merger with a better-placed society. With the backing of the union and the society's management committee, he entered into talks with the Leek and Moorlands whose position under the Act was completely secure.

The successful outcome not only added the £13 million of NALGO funds to the Leek and Moorlands £46 million. It also gave the Leek and Moorlands a London office for the first time. Lees was appointed assistant general manager with responsibility for the London operation.

Special terms were agreed to preserve the benefits of the NALGO society's members. There was a guarantee of a mortgage rate a quarter per cent lower than that recommended by The Building Societies Association. And the Leek and Moorlands guaranteed to make available to NALGO members one fifth of the capital it lent annually and to retain an office in the NALGO headquarters building so that Lees could continue to give personal service to members. The union also had its own insurance company, and, as a by-product of the agreement, the company retained its monopoly of fire insurance of every freehold house bought by a NALGO member through the Leek and Moorlands, and of the member's life cover when this was required.

The union's newspaper, Public Service, commented on the deal: "Billy Lloyd's 'baby' has grown to man's estate. In wedlock, he should thrive and prosper". The deal was certainly a success. In 1960, the Leek and Moorlands lent £2 million to NALGO members. As the union's official history of the period records, this was £500,000 more than the NALGO Building Society could have done, and on terms a quarter per cent cheaper. Clearly, the stability and security offered by lending to local government and public industry officers was an attractive prospect for the Leek and Moorlands. Equally attractive was the low expense of the NALGO operation and the low volume of correspondence and paper work. To this day, a presence is maintained in the NALGO headquarters. The Leek helped in the financing of the new NALGO headquarters opened on 7th May, 1976, in Mabledon Place, off Euston Road in London. The Leek, now in the form of the Britannia Building Society, has a splendid office fronting the Euston Road, between the major London stations of Euston, St. Pancras and Kings Cross.

The House Purchase and Housing Act brought a second society into the Leek fold — the 85-year-old Atlas Building Society of Stockport. Its assets totalled £350,000. Like the NALGO Building Society, it was a sound concern although ineligible for trustee status. Hubert Newton commented: "The finances of this society are strong and its underlying property security is first-class". The transfer of assets took place on 30th September, 1960.

The impact of the 1959 House Purchase and Housing Act had had an effect on the Leek and Moorlands that it could not have anticipated. But of greater importance to the whole building society movement was the Building Societies Act, 1960, whose significance lay in the fact that it legally transformed building societies into the owner-occupier housing finance organisations they are today.

The Act followed the difficulties revealed in the movement at the end of the 1950s and severely limited the proportion of a society's lending which could be devoted to objects other than home ownership. It gave the Registrar of Friendly Societies wider powers to protect the public. The Act, consolidated in another Act of 1962, provided the framework for the movement's operations for years to come.

Building societies up to the 1960 Act had freedom to choose the kind of property their loans were secured on, as long as the property was freehold or leasehold. Building societies had traditionally lent much of their money on rented property, shops and even industrial premises.

Although the inter-war surge in home ownership had altered the balance of lending, the societies did not see themselves as just institutions for home ownership. The Leek and Moorlands, more than most, stressed the value of home ownership in its reports and was stronger than most in this field, but it still lent extensively in other areas.

But this general freedom was exploited by small unscrupulous societies who wanted to grow quickly by speculative lending. This was, of course, against the spirit of the movement itself. It also had the practical effect of taking away money from home ownership at a time of heavy demand. The 1960 Act arose out of the feeling that something must be done to limit this other kind of lending.

What the Act did was to divide loans into two kinds — special advances and normal advances. Special advances covered commercial loans and loans of above £5,000 to an individual. No more than ten per cent of a building society's lending could be in special advances. The normal advances, accounting for 90 per cent, could still be for rented property or commercial property but as the demand in these sectors for such small loans was low, the change meant that the overwhelming total of a building society's lending now had to go into owner-occupation. Societies in future years were in fact reluctant to go anywhere near the ten per cent level in special advances. The £5,000 limit has since been raised several times to keep pace with rapidly rising house prices.

The Act also established several other basic new principles. Directors and officers were not allowed to make mortgage reports and valuations because of potential conflict of interest, although a ten-year period of grace was allowed for existing directors and officers before the ban took place. People founding societies now had to have a financial stake in them. Ten members, each investing at least £500 each, were required to get a new society off the ground. The minimum level of liquid funds to be eligible for trustee status was raised to 7.5 per cent and the eligible liquid investments closely defined both as to type — local authority loans, Treasury bills and gilt-edged — and to dates of maturity. The rights of members in a society were strengthened both in the inspection of records and in participation at meetings.

The Act also laid down legal guidelines by which societies could help others in difficulty. The Chief Registrar was given power to authorise the lending of funds between societies, and the movement was empowered to set up a guarantee fund to meet losses suffered by investors or depositors in a society subscribing to the fund. This power was not then, in fact, taken up. The societies feared it might encourage the reckless kind of lending by smaller societies which the Act was designed to deter.

Above all, the Chief Registrar's control over societies was greatly strengthened. He could now call for a meeting or an inspection of the books without having to wait for members to ask him. And he was now given total power to prevent a society taking new investments.

Meanwhile, other more local concerns occupied the attention of the Leek and Moorlands. 1960 saw the jubilee celebrations of the City of Stoke-on-Trent, and a 50-mile walk was held to commemorate the jubilee. The winner was Miss Hilda Mellor, a member of the Leek and Moorlands chief office staff. Further extensions were completed during the year to the New Stockwell House headquarters.

At the annual general meeting on 10th April, 1961, Sir Ernest Johnson resigned as President. He had taken on the post in 1938, and had seen the funds grow from £6,300,000 to £63,000,000. Mr Gilbert Tatton, the board chairman, succeeded him. Sadly Gilbert Tatton's tenure of the presidency was to be a short one. He died early the next year at 73, after serving 17 years as chairman and 22 as a director. Both Johnson and Tatton were men very much part of the North Staffordshire industrial scene in the old tradition of the society. Johnson had been managing director of Johnson Bros (Hanley) Ltd, who claimed to be the largest firm of earthenware manufacturers in the world. He was one-time president of the British Pottery Manufacturers Association. Tatton's career comprised both the managing directorship of the Leek dyeing company, Sir Thomas and Arthur Wardle, and the chairmanship and managing directorship of Leek Chemicals.

Into the Leek and Moorlands in 1961 came three more small building societies — the Radcliffe Building Society, the Congleton Equitable Benefit Building Society and a second Stockport society, the Stockport and East Cheshire Permanent Benefit Building Society. The Radcliffe transfer took place on 30th June, 1961. The Radcliffe had been founded in 1873 and its assets now totalled £603,298. The acquisition gave the Leek and Moorlands a branch in Radcliffe. The Congleton Equitable came in on 30th September. It had been established in 1854 and its assets were £466,863. The Stockport merger was announced in November although the formal transfer took place on 31st December. The Stockport and East Cheshire's assets were £87,956. It had been founded in 1877.

Although the Leek and Moorlands had taken over two Stockport societies in such a short space of time, its links with the town were longstanding. It had been represented there for nearly 40 years, firstly as an agency through Messrs Garner and Son — in fact, the society's first agency — and then in 1959 through the opening of a branch office.

A notable event in 1961 came on 27th October when the society played host in Yorkshire to the England and Staffordshire cricketer, S. F. Barnes, who performed the opening ceremony of the new branch office at Keighley.

The early 1960s were good years for building societies, but national economic problems had repercussions. In July, 1961, Bank Rate jumped from five to seven per cent. Then it was reduced in stages to 4.5 per cent by April, 1962. Building societies' rates had gone up the month before the jump in Bank Rate, but as Bank Rate dropped, so the societies faced criticism for not reducing their rates. For ten years, societies had not had enough cash to keep pace with mortgage demand yet the pressure was now on them to follow closely the national movement in interest rates and risk depressing the inflow of funds.

Newton had backed the rise in building society rates in June, 1961. At the Leek and Moorlands annual luncheon in May, 1961, at Stoke, he pointed out the increased administrative burdens on building societies from the 1960 Act and other changes in the financial system. Despite these new burdens, societies still faced very keen competition for savings from the government and other financial institutions.

Pointing out that the National Savings movement gained tax-free advantages for its investors, Newton asked: "Why not give building societies similar tax-free advantages for their investors?" He told the luncheon that the remedy lay with the government — to ease building society taxation and/or to reduce the yields on national savings. "If neither of these courses suit Government policy", then borrowers might have to face another increase.

The Leek and Moorlands had followed The Building Societies Association recommendation in June to raise the share rate by 0.25 per cent to 3.75 per cent. But it stepped out of line with the other societies by freezing its rate on existing mortgages instead of increasing them by 0.5 per cent to 6.5 per cent. The rate of interest on new mortgages was increased. The freeze was a sign of the Leek's strength. The bold decision was also helped by a capital profit on the resale of the society's premises in Nottingham.

Newton was one of the strongest opponents in the movement to the idea that its investment rates should fall again as interest rates eased generally in 1962. In a public statement in May, 1962, he said he favoured providing loans as cheaply as possible but maintained that there was one thing more important than cheaper home loans: "It is to make sure that such loans are freely and fully available". The only way to cheapen loans was, he said, by cutting interest rates to investors but such a move would bring less money into the societies for mortgages.

It was not until January, 1963, that The Building Societies Association decided to recommend a reduction, to come into effect in April. The new rates were six per cent for mortgages and 3.5 per cent for share accounts. However, the Leek board meeting in January agreed to differ. It brought in the six per cent rate in February. But the share rate remained unaltered despite the BSA recommendation. At that time, the biggest society, the Halifax, was outside the BSA and the Leek's moves were taken in the light of this competitive situation. In September, the board agreed to bring in the 3.5 per cent share rate from January, 1964.

July 1962 saw another important boost to the growing national status of the Leek and Moorlands. New premises were opened on the 17th of the month at Kingsway in London. They gave the Leek a branch office in London in addition to its regional office at NALGO House. New branch offices were also opened in Nottingham and Derby during the year.

The need for new London offices had been evident for some time. The board hoped it might be possible to take over a small society with London premises but no such opportunity turned up. The Leek and Moorlands had now had a presence in the capital for 30 years, working mostly through local sole agents.

Newton made an interesting comment in an interview with the *Financial Times* about the London moves. He told the paper that there was no question at this time of changing the society's "rather parochial title". He said much goodwill was associated with the present name, and the fact that the society was closely linked with a small Staffordshire town of 20,000 people had not hindered its growth.

July 1962 also saw important board changes following on the death of Gilbert Tatton. The deputy chairman, Sir Bernard White, was appointed president of the society and chairman of the board. Hubert Newton, director, general manager, and secretary of the society, now became the deputy chairman as well. On 26th November, his executive designation was amended to that of managing director and secretary.

In 1962, Newton was elected president of the International Union of Building Societies at its Washington Convention. He became only the third person in the British building society movement to have held both the posts of chairman of The Building Societies Association and president of the International Union. The others were Enoch Hill of the Halifax and Harold Bellman of the Abbey Road. Figures presented to the convention emphasised the strength of the International Union. At the time of Newton's accession to the presidency, it represented 60 million savers in 28 countries, and home loans and savings of over £80 billion. He served as president until the 1965 World Congress in London.

The question of computerisation was now beginning to exercise the Leek and Moorlands directors' minds as the volume and complexity of the society's work grew. The first reference crops up in the board minutes of 14th January, 1963. No action was taken at this time.

On 26th July, 1963, an opening ceremony was held for the new branch office in Altrincham, Cheshire. The guest was the President of the Board of Trade, the Rt Hon Frederick Errol. Other new offices were opened during the year at Burslem in April, Huddersfield in November, and Wood Green in London in December.

The internal expansion of 1963 gave way once more to external expansion in 1964 when more small societies came into the Leek and Moorlands fold. On 1st January, the Kidderminster Mutual Building Society was absorbed. It dated from 1876 and its assets totalled £218,893. On 1st April, the Aylesbury Permanent Building Society was absorbed. It dated from 1871. Its assets were £457,397. On 1st July, the Leek and Moorlands acquired what was really its first London society, if the NALGO society is regarded as a national union society. The society taken over on that date was the Lion Building Society of Chislehurst in Kent. Chislehurst had just switched administratively from Kent to the new Greater London area. And the Lion, besides its head office in Chislehurst, also brought with it an office in Moorgate in the City of London. A third Lion office was in Reading. The Lion ranked behind the NALGO acquisition as the Leek's second biggest takeover up to that time. Assets were £5,205,820 and they swelled the total assets of the Leek and Moorlands to over £100 million. The Leek and Moorlands now held the position of ninth largest building society.

The Lion was a comparative newcomer to the movement. It was founded in 1937 and was one of the larger of the "independent" societies who were not members of The Building Societies Association. It also had an extensive network of agents in southern England. The move was seen by the Leek as a highly significant step in its growing penetration of the South where housing development and population growth were going ahead much more quickly than in the rest of the country.

In July, 1964, Sir Bernard White died and he was followed in the

New Stockwell House Centenary Celebrations 1956

A Silver Salver being presented by the Society's President Sir Ernest Johnson (right) to Gilbert Tatton, Chairman of the Board of Directors, and given by the Agents of the Society as a token of their esteem and association.

Centenary Luncheon at the North Stafford Hotel, Stoke-on-Trent, 31st May, 1956.

Transfer of Engagements. Newcastle-under-Lyme Benefit Building Society and Stone New Freehold Benefit Building Society to Leek & Moorlands Building Society, 1957. Left to right: A. Ravenscroft (Stone), K. A. Morgan (Newcastle), R. Goodill (Stone), Sir Bernard White (Leek), Sir Ernest Johnson (Leek), Hubert Newton (Leek), G. Tatton (Leek), A. Morgan (Newcastle).

Transfer of Engagements. Newcastle (Staffs) & District Building Society to Leek & Moorlands Building Society, 1958. Left to right: W. Parton (Newcastle), S. Myott (Leek), Hubert Newton (Leek), E. Corbishley (Newcastle), J. Legge (Newcastle), Sir Bernard White (Leek), G. Tatton (Leek), R. Statham (Newcastle), G. L. Walley (Newcastle), Alderman Ramsbottom (Newcastle), Sir Ernest Johnson (Leek), F. Morris (Newcastle), J. Waite (Newcastle).

chairmanship by Hubert Newton. The title of president was dropped and so Newton became the titular head of the society whose fortunes he had so successfully led for three decades. In memory of Sir Bernard, the board decided to provide a prize to be awarded annually to the student obtaining the best marks in the examination of The Building Societies Institute in law and practice.

The change coincided with another difficult time for the Leek and Moorlands as once more it found itself seriously out of step with The Building Societies Association. The return of the first Labour government for 13 years saw many new proposals for housing finance, including lower interest rates for future owner-occupiers.

One proposal by George Brown, the deputy Labour leader, was for mortgages to be granted at three per cent. Hubert Newton discounted this specific figure but put forward in public his own view that Brown was really thinking of taxation relief for building societies with specific government help, as a way of reducing the cost of mortgages.

"He could well have had in mind a scheme whereby building societies lend 95 per cent, and 50 per cent of the loan could be building society money at current home rates and the remaining 45 per cent could be interest-free or low interest rate money loaned by the Government to building societies".

But Newton added this warning, if such a policy were not forthcoming:

"If National Savings are to receive a shot in the arm, which means either a higher interest rate or some further tax concessions, or both, building societies, in the absence of similar concessions, will have to take defensive measures to protect their funds. This will mean an increase in both rates of interest — for savings and home loans".

The plans of the government soon had to be put on one side because of the worsening financial situation and the general world rise in interest rates. It was not until 1967 when the government brought in the Housing Subsidies Act to help low-income borrowers that any of its plans came to fruition.

But the fears of Newton on building society interest rates were to materialise only too quickly. By October, 1964, the societies were finding their business falling off. A rise in rates was now considered. This was, of course, very unwelcome to the government. It had dangled before the electors' eyes the prospect of cheaper rates. Now rates looked set to rise after only a few months in office. Government pressure which included a meeting by the Chancellor of the Exchequer, James Callaghan, and the Minister of Housing, Richard Crossman, with the Council of The Building Societies Association, succeeded in deferring the rise for the time being. But it left societies facing a tide of withdrawals. Income tax changes did not help, adding 5d. to the special composite rate paid to the government, with the prospect of another 5d. the next year. The 5d. rise brought the rate to 5s. 10d.

The Leek and Moorlands, under Newton, was not prepared to wait. At the November monthly meeting of the Council, Newton made clear his disagreement with the policy. Newton had received the prior backing of his board at a meeting on 9th November. The board decided that the society should withdraw from the interest rates undertaking and that Newton should be relieved of his personal undertaking as a Council member.

The board made clear its feeling that any other course of action would play into the hands of those societies who were formally acknowledging the undertaking but bypassing it in other ways. It was an issue on which Newton particularly felt strongly. Throughout his career, he had always opposed the unfairness of policies that were not applied to all.

Although the Leek and Moorlands had taken the lead in the opposition to the Association's policy, it was not the first to put up its rates. The Leicester Permanent was the first, and the Leek followed along with the other Leicester society, the Leicester Temperance.

The Leek board resolved at its meeting on 21st December that the share rate be raised to 3.75 per cent. Rates of interest to new borrowers were to be 6.75 per cent but there was no increase for existing borrowers. The new rates were to come in on 1st January, 1965.

During 1964, the Leek had advanced a record mortgage total of £21,500,000 but had had to impose restrictions on mortgage lending because demand had outstripped its supply of cash under the old interest rate structure.

Shortly afterwards, the Association was forced to come to terms with the logic of events recognised by the Leek and the Leicester societies. At the January meeting of the Council, the same rise in interest rates was recommended to the movement as a whole. But the situation remained an unstable one. Although the higher interest rates paid out brought in more receipts, withdrawals also increased. Net receipts for the movement in the first half of 1965 were to fall by one-third compared with the same period in 1964.

1964 was also a major year for branch office expansion. Offices were opened at Bath, Bournemouth, Crewe, Ilford, Guildford and Nantwich to give the Leek and Moorlands an even broader national base, and in the Potteries themselves at Meir, Tunstall and Stoke. The society's growing business also meant the addition during the year of more extensions to New Stockwell House. These were followed in 1965 by the building in the grounds at the rear of New Stockwell House of the first official staff canteen. The canteen was formally opened on 28th May by Mrs Harold Ball, wife of a former assistant secretary to the society.

The worrying situation over interest rates led to Newton issuing a number of national warnings. In March, 1965, a branch was opened at Taunton, the formal ceremony being undertaken by the town's MP, Mr Edward Du Cann. Newton spoke at the ceremony of "a complete lack of confidence in the situation" among the movement. The price for money internationally was on the increase, he pointed out, and warned mortgage borrowers that they could not look forward to "much reduction this year, indeed, if any at all".

At the Leek and Moorlands annual luncheon in Stoke on 6th May, he returned to the theme. House buyers, he said, should be told they would have to wait until the economic position was restored before they could expect loans at low interest rates. He called on the government to be equally forthright:

"Either the squeeze is necessary to the whole economy or it is phoney. Why not tell the truth and make it clear that in the present situation, would-be home buyers will have to wait?"

At that time, the Housing Minister, Richard Crossman, was negotiating with the building societies over his target of 500,000 new houses a year by 1970. He wanted a half-half mix between local authority and private housing. In 1964, houses built by local authorities had totalled just 126,000 against 221,000 for the private sector. Quite clearly, any half-half agreement would probably mean the building societies having to rein in their lending.

Some societies appeared willing to go along with self-imposed restriction but the idea annoyed Newton. He spoke at the luncheon of a Crossman reference to "the whim of the investor" in housebuilding. The minister, said Newton, overlooked the "whim" of the investor which had enabled the building societies to provide, at no cost to the government, a not inconsiderable supply of home finance.

"If building societies were to satisfy the 'whim' of the investor today, they would be paying much higher rates. They would, however, be in company with local authorities which are lending at seven and 7.25 per cent".

Crossman's housing ambitions were to disappear with the collapse of the Labour Government's economic plans as enshrined in its National Plan. Crisis measures were to come in the following year, 1966, bringing the biggest deflationary package seen in post-war Britain, and a price, wage, and dividend freeze.

But Newton's warning in that month of May, 1965, was soon to be backed by more controversial action. On 26th May, 1965, he announced that the Leek and Moorlands was unilaterally increasing its rate to investors to four per cent.

The news of the Leek and Moorlands action came as a bombshell because the previous week the conference of The Building Societies Association at Brighton had decided overwhelmingly to hold to 3.75 per cent for share investment and 6.75 per cent for mortgages. The members had assumed the subject was closed — at least until the next Council meeting on 11th June.

Newton had now put the Association in a very awkward position. It had decided not to increase rates because it felt that an extra 0.25 per cent would not be enough to bring in the funds needed to solve the serious situation the societies were facing. And it would require an increase in the mortgage rate, which they felt undesirable in the political situation, or a cut in margins. A cut in margins would embarrassingly have contradicted an assurance given to the Chancellor the previous December that the societies had no option but to increase their margins because of higher taxation.

Newton's decisive position on interest rates had again forced him into the forefront of controversy. Yet at the same time, he was an acknowledged leader of the movement, having led his own society for more than 30 years and having held many top positions in the movement. Venerable leaders were not supposed to act in the way he was doing. A look at how the *Financial Times* economics correspondent of the day and its Men and Matters column dealt with the Leek and Moorlands decision and with Newton personally, gives some idea of the tremendous national impact he was making.

The economics correspondent, George Cyriax, pointed out just how well placed the Leek and Moorlands was to take this kind of initiative. It had a high reserve ratio of 4.9 per cent and was "well placed to absorb the lower margin and extra interest cost for a while". But he warned of "serious friction" within The Building Societies Association over Newton's move:

"Mr Newton, though a consistent advocate of higher rates, is also on the Association's Council, is a past chairman — with the right this gives in selecting a new chairman — and is president of the International

Union of Building Societies. There is a general feeling that he should not have acted on his own, in opposition to the Council's decision on recommended interest rates a week ago.

"Indeed, there is a growing question in the movement about the whole role of the Association's recommended rate of interest. One third of societies by number — mostly the smaller ones — already pay above the recommended rates and, with some larger societies such as the Leek and Moorlands going their own way, the advantages of feeling tied to the recommended rate have noticeably declined".

It is doubtful whether Newton has ever let a sense of position and power in the movement deflect him from his basic beliefs. The article in Men and Matters was a good deal less reproving than that of the economics correspondent and it caught more exactly the character of Hubert Newton. It is worth quoting in full because of this:

"In the scale of emotive words, mortgage ranks only just under home and children these days. Leek and Moorlands may be only the tenth biggest building society, and be a difficult name to remember, but it was bound to get itself some big black headlines by being the first to raise its deposit rates. But in a movement that sometimes seems almost neurotically shy, Mr Hubert Newton, L and M's chairman, is that rarity, a man with both a taste and a talent for publicity.

"A year ago, he warned The Building Societies Association that he might want to raise his deposit rates; soon after, he warned that he might even do it without giving the customary 28 days' notice to the BSA. A week ago, he argued forcefully at the BSA annual conference that they should all raise their rates — homebuyers would be harmed more by lack of mortgages than by paying more for them, though he says at the moment that he will not have to charge more. Despite his stature in the movement (he is a big man in the BSA and head of the international body), the delegates were unconvinced; there was quite a row. Yesterday's announcement was probably inevitable.

"Of course, Newton could have broken the news more gently; were things really so urgent that he could not wait 28 days? BSA gossips murmur that the L and M has suffered more than most from depositors' withdrawals, which is probably just a bit of backbiting. The reason is more likely to be in Newton's character. A tough Northerner from Burnley (why do so many building society chiefs come from Burnley?), he started in the movement at 14, and joined the L and M 30 years ago. Its deposits were then £3.5 million; they are now £106 million.

"That rate of growth does not come from quiet plodding, and the

L and M, though still based in Staffordshire, has spread both north and south, partly through shrewd acquisitions of less aggressive societies. Like Lord Cohen of the Alliance, Newton clearly sees a building society more as a business than as a benevolent fund, which makes good sense. Unlike Cohen, he sees himself more as a rebel, with the role of waking up more slothful societies, which he does with both charm and success.

"Perhaps, though, the head of a society with a name like Leek and Moorlands needs to do something to make it stick in the mind".

Newton's lead was followed by a number of other societies, and, faced with this situation, the Council of The Building Societies Association was compelled to change its position. At the meeting on 11th June, it recommended members to increase the share rate to four per cent from 1st July. The Council added that in the light of prevailing conditions, it did not intend to recommend an increase in the mortgage rate even though working margins would now be reduced.

The societies were to be stuck with reduced margins for some time. A rise to seven per cent in the mortgage rate when the rate had already been increased to 6.75 per cent, would have provoked deep hostility from the government. The days of frequently changing rates were still a decade away. Before the September meeting of the Council, the BSA chairman, Donald Gould, had talks with the Chancellor, James Callaghan, who specifically asked that no further change in the mortgage rate be made. The Council at the September meeting believed it had no choice but to persevere with the reduced margins.

In the meantime, Newton was strongly pushing his own view that the BSA should no longer be pursuing a policy of common recommended rates. He outlined his ideas at a press reception in London on 29th June:

"It is the view of my Board that in certain matters, it should be free to operate any reasonable policy best suited to the requirements and financial soundness of the Leek and Moorlands.

"The recent contretemps regarding interest rates show the impracticality of trying to establish a recommended rate. If Board policy is to be governed by a series of printed notices issued from 14 Park Street (headquarters of the Association), Boards may as well surrender their duties forthwith and relinquish their offices.

"There are many things which an Association can and should do but it should think twice before it seeks to abrogate to itself those duties which are essentially a matter for individual Boards of directors".

Newton extended his attack on the existing system to the traditional conception of reserve funds of building societies, which on average amounted to four per cent. "There are times when we ought to think of using reserves for the benefit of members instead of thinking that year by year, they are something to be kept in cold storage".

Meanwhile, Newton had many other activities on his plate, as a man with interests in so many parts of the building society world. In April and June, he attended meetings of the European Federation of Building Societies at which it was agreed to admit The Building Societies Association to membership. A five-day working week for Leek and Moorlands staff and an improved annual holiday scheme were agreed by Newton and the board. The scheme still kept open counters on Saturday morning. A new social activity was inaugurated in October, when a golf tournament was held on the Leek golf course for friends of the society in North Staffordshire. The event was to become an annual one. A staff social club was formed at the Leek headquarters.

Branches were opened during the year at Bangor, Brighton, Buxton, Southport, Wilmslow, and Newcastle (Staffs) as well as Taunton.

In October, the International Union of Building Societies and Savings and Loans Associations held its congress at the Hilton Hotel in London. Newton as president accompanied Princess Margaret when she performed the opening ceremony. Nearly 1,000 delegates from 36 countries attended the week long convention. This made it the largest international gathering ever of building society people. Among those who gave addresses was the Prime Minister, Harold Wilson, who gave fulsome praise to the movement at home and abroad.

The occasion gave immense personal satisfaction to Newton who had planned it over the years of his presidency. His grand-daughter, Annabel Ross, was present to give Princess Margaret a bouquet and there was a personal connection in this. Annabel's father had been son of a factor at Balmoral during the reign of King George VI, and Princess Margaret as a child knew him well. On the last day, Newton was presented by the congress with a study in oils by Van Bloemart. The Leek and Moorlands marked its own recognition of Newton's presidency when Lt-Col Worthington presented to the union a collar and jewel to be worn by succeeding presidents.

But despite such intense activity throughout 1965 at the highest levels of the building society movement, Newton found time to plan his biggest move yet for the Leek and Moorlands — a merger with the London-based Westbourne Park Building Society. The deal, announced on 1st September, not only brought with it the £53 million assets of the Westbourne. It also meant the Leek losing its much cherished "Moorlands" title which it had carried right from its beginnings in 1856. The merged societies took the name of Leek and Westbourne. The formal amalgamation and change of name was to come into effect on 31st December.

The combined assets of the two societies totalled £179 million, making the merger the second biggest in British building society history — after the merger of the Abbey Road and National societies in 1944. It put the Leek into sixth place in the national table of building societies, based on asset totals, behind the Halifax, Abbey National, Co-operative Permanent, Woolwich Equitable and Leeds Permanent. The new operation was to have joint chief offices — at Leek and at the Westbourne Park's headquarters, Westbourne House, Westbourne Grove, London.

The merger strengthened the Leek's southern base considerably. The Westbourne Park society's operations had been mainly confined to the south of England, where it had 17 branch offices, many on the south coast. In only two towns did the societies' offices duplicate — Luton and Bournemouth. The total number of branches of the combined societies totalled 75.

The chairman of the Westbourne Park was Lord Hurd, formerly Sir Anthony Hurd, who had been Conservative MP for Newbury in Berkshire, until he was made a life peer in 1964. Its managing director was Mr Edward Moody.

It was through his good relations with Moody that Newton had engineered the merger. But although he was the driving force, he was content to take a titular back seat for the sake of future harmony within the merged society. Lord Hurd was to be chairman of the Leek and Westbourne with Newton as deputy chairman. Newton was to be joint managing director with Moody.

The Westbourne was a smaller society — 17th in the assets table — but it brought with it a tremendous potential which Newton had recognised. Recent slow growth had built up a liquidity ratio of 27.8 per cent — enormously high for a building society, and probably the highest in the movement at the time.

The merger was part of an increasing trend in the movement to amalgamation. Only two years before, the Bradford and Bingley societies had merged their operations to create a society of £114 million in assets. The latest report of the Chief Registrar of Friendly Societies showed that the number of societies at the end of 1964 — 635 — had been reduced by 97 over the previous five years.

Concentration gave economies of scale in operation. It gave a geographical spread of business which helped societies stabilise their movement of funds in and out. And it enabled societies to spend the amounts needed on marketing to make them household names to whom the public would turn. One further specific advantage was that societies with over £100 million assets only needed to put two per cent of their funds above that figure into reserves to qualify for trustee status. The smaller societies required 2.5 per cent.

The argument of economies of scale was growing stronger as computerisation began to make its appearance. The crediting of yearly and half-yearly interest, the arrangement of a flexible system of withdrawals and deposits, and the handling of a large number of fairly standardised mortgage requests were all ideal fodder for the computer. Already the five largest societies ahead of the Leek and Westbourne were installing or planning to install their first computers.

Even after this large merger, Newton was not finished. On 8th November, the Leek and Westbourne took over the Penistone Building Society and its assets of £632,543, so establishing a Leek and Westbourne branch office in the West Yorkshire town. The Penistone society dated back to 1867.

The Leek and Westbourne merger was approved at a special general meeting of Leek and Moorlands members at the Town Hall, Leek, on Monday, 26th October. The voting by poll was: For (including proxy votes) 10,254; Against 28; Spoiled papers 1.

Like the Leek, the Westbourne Park had become a national name in the pre-war period and it was a society with an equally distinguished history. Whereas many societies had been founded in Victorian times by workmen meeting in pubs, the Westbourne had a rather different origin — in a church — and it retained this religious connection over much of its separate life.

The church was the Westbourne Park Baptist Church in West London. The society was formed in 1885 at a meeting of church deacons and church workers. The prime mover of the idea was the church pastor, the Rev Dr John Clifford, who was first president of the society and its leading light for many years.

The proposal put before the meeting was that the society should be started "as a help and inducement for the young people connected with the church to cultivate thrift and to provide the means whereby they could secure their own homes".

The date of the meeting was 30th July, and 19 people are recorded as being present, described as "mostly young men". The chief office of the new society was set up in the schoolroom of the church.

Alongside John Clifford, the first chairman of the Westbourne Park was Mr E. Cayford, a partner in the shipping firm of Houlder Bros, and afterwards chairman of the shipping company bearing that name. He only stayed in the chair for a year but it was his practical expertise which enabled the society to be launched. He did much work in helping prepare and then examine the draft rules, and also in laying down general business methods of operation.

The first secretary was Mr C. Johnson Burt, who made the Westbourne Park very much of a family affair. His daughter, Miss Violet Johnson Burt, was his assistant for many years. He held the post until 1929. His successor, Mr George Jeffries, was to become the first general manager. Jeffries was succeeded in 1946 by Mr Arthur Halton, who had been at one time with the Leek and Moorlands. Mr Edward Moody was the third general manager of the society, taking up his post in 1960. Moody had started off his career with the former London-based National society, now part of the Abbey National. He joined the Westbourne Park in 1945 as staff manager, becoming assistant secretary in 1946 and assistant general manager in 1951. He became a board member in 1964. He was a freeman of the City of London, and, like Newton, a prominent Rotarian.

The original solicitors to the Westbourne Park, T. Richards and Company, remained with it throughout its existence, and were retained by the merged society.

The Westbourne area took its name from a small London river, the Westbourne, long since covered over, which flows into the Serpentine.

In 1889, the Westbourne Park society moved to more regular office premises at 56 Porchester Road, followed by a second move in 1899 to 136 Westbourne Terrace. Dr Clifford was a leading non-conformist of the time, and the society was governed from the first by very strict rules. When the 1894 Building Societies Act was brought in, the Westbourne Park had already anticipated its provisions many years before. In the Victorian era, many societies made their money by large industrial advances. The Westbourne refused to enter into this kind of business, keeping its lending local and domestic.

Its growth in the inter-war years saw it open large modern offices at Westbourne House, Westbourne Grove, London W2, in 1931. These offices were to become the joint head office of the Leek and Westbourne.

In its time, the Westbourne Park had taken over three societies, the Ashford (Kent) Permanent, the Railway Permanent, and the Lloyds Permanent. The Lloyds Permanent had only joined the Westbourne at the start of 1965.

The first meeting of the new combined board took place at Westbourne House. Two local committees for Leek and London were appointed and the powers of the joint managing directors set out. The following executive staff were appointed: joint general managers, Mr N. Cowburn (previously Leek and Moorlands), Mr E. A. W. Kempson (previously Westbourne Park); joint deputy general managers, Mr J. C. Ainsworth (previously Leek and Moorlands), Mr S. L. Masters (previously Westbourne Park); assistant general manager, Mr G. H. Lees (previously Leek and Moorlands); chief accountant, Mr J. W. Webb (previously Leek and Moorlands); joint secretaries, Mr L. Beardmore (previously Leek and Moorlands), Mr J. C. Chaplin (previously Westbourne Park); branches and agencies manager, Mr J. Quipp (previously Leek and Moorlands).

The board also took what was to be a momentous decision for the future. The growing size of the old Leek and Moorlands operation plus the extra work following on the merger made the existing head offices set-up inadequate. So the board took the decision to look for land in Leek to build a new headquarters.

It agreed first to look into the possibility of acquiring land on the Barnfields Industrial Estate in Leek. Later that year, in March, outline planning permission was refused, but negotiations were set in hand for a site of 20 acres in Cheadle Road, Leek. They were ultimately successful.

The advent of the new society was marred by the death soon afterwards of its chairman, Lord Hurd. On the 8th February, 1966, he left the country for a stay in Antigua. He died there suddenly on 12th February. At a meeting of the board on 29th March, 1966, Newton was appointed chairman and Moody deputy chairman. So Newton, who had generously yielded the chairmanship to Lord Hurd at the merger once again took on the formal mantle of leadership.

8: A New Home

OTHER MERGERS RAPIDLY followed in 1966 on the Westbourne merger. Soon after the acquisition of the Penistone Building Society, yet another acquisition was announced — that of the Orient Permanent Building Society of Brentwood in Essex, with assets of £1.25 million. It was absorbed on 1st January, 1966, the same day as the Leek and Westbourne came into formal existence. It dated from 1880. On 1st March, 1966, the Crewe Permanent Benefit Building Society, with assets of £600,000, was taken into the new grouping. It dated from 1867. The Newton philosophy of growth by absorption was now at its height.

The annual meeting was held at the Porchester Hall, Paddington, on 20th April, 1966. Leek Town Hall — the home of the Leek and Moorlands annual meeting down the decades — must have seemed strangely desolate that day. Newton pointed out that the Leek and Westbourne was now the product of 22 different societies. He added:

"The Society is always prepared to discuss the possibility of mergers with Societies whose Directors and Members seek to obtain the benefits which can accrue from this form of expansion".

The year was to see two more societies taken in — both of them from the town of Glossop in Derbyshire. The Longdendale Permanent Benefit Building Society of Glossop was absorbed on 31st October and the Glossop Perpetual Building Society the following day — 1st November. Both were societies with similar histories, the Longdendale starting life in 1877 and the Glossop Perpetual in 1875. The Longdendale had assets of £272,219 and the Glossop Perpetual assets of £218,527.

Another takeover took place the following year in very difficult and different circumstances. The building society was the troubled Alliance Perpetual which had run into problems several years back and had been barred since 1960 from advertising for new deposits.

The Leek and Westbourne became involved with the Alliance Perpetual shortly after its own formation. The Alliance Perpetual, a society dating back to 1854, was based at 46 Baker Street, London. Its directors approached Hubert Newton for help and advice, and asked him to recommend someone to take over its management. A new board had been appointed in 1961 under the chairmanship of Sir Charles Norton to put the society's affairs in order but it was still a tremendous struggle. The name of Edward Kempson, the joint general manager of the Leek and Westbourne and formerly of the Westbourne Park, was put forward by Newton. Kempson, due to retire on 31st October, was released on secondment.

In fact, his secondment was a prelude to the takeover of the Alliance Perpetual. In June 1967, Newton was co-opted to the board as the representative of the Leek and Westbourne, and the takeover was announced for the end of the year. The Alliance Perpetual had assets of £7 million, and so successful had been the turnround in its affairs that Newton was able to announce that "no one has lost one penny either of capital or interest".

This takeover followed the takeover in 1967 of two smaller societies, the Acme and National Independent Permanent Benefit societies. The National Independent was based in Manchester and was taken over on 31st March. It had assets of £345,453. It was an even older society than the Leek and Moorlands, having been founded in 1853. The Acme was a tiny London society, based at Upper Holloway, with assets of just £61,664. In complete contrast to the National Independent, it had been founded 100 years later — in 1953. It came in on 1st May, 1967.

In September 1966, the Leek and Westbourne finally got the site it wanted for its new headquarters. The purchase of the land in Cheadle Road, Leek, was successfully completed. Land comprising 13 acres was bought from Messrs J. & R. Beech for £15,000, and another 24 acres, including 14 acres of woodland, was bought from Lt-Col W. J. Challinor, the last remaining vice-president of the society, for £17,500. Planning permission had been obtained earlier for the development. He died the following year, so ending the vice presidential post in the society.

The Cheadle Road site was a great contrast to the central position of New Stockwell House in the crowded town centre of Leek close to the market place. It was in the countryside on the fringes of the town, on steeply sloping ground, backed by rising woodland to the east and overlooking the Churnet valley to the west and the hills beyond. To the north was a view of Leek, with church towers and roofs seen through the trees.

The architects appointed to design the new headquarters were Messrs Adams and Green of Stoke-on-Trent. A hectic time of planning lay ahead for the Leek and Westbourne until the completion of the project four years later. Meetings took place throughout 1967 on the details of the project — with the architects, surveyors and others. At a board meeting in November, a tender of £107,866 by C. Cornes and Son Limited of Stoke-on-Trent and London for the main contracting work was accepted.

It was agreed that work should start without delay and Mrs Newton cut the first sod of turf in December. The Leek and Westbourne owed a considerable debt of gratitude to Leek's MP, Mr Harold Davies. At that time, building licences were in force because of the national economic problems, and Davies did a lot of work to ease the passage of the vital licence.

The pressing need for the new headquarters had been shown in December 1966, when the Leek and Westbourne was forced to purchase additional office space in Leek for the mortgage department. The property bought was the Milward Hall, in Strangman Street, and internal alterations were carried out to make it suitable.

The design of the new headquarters was to be linked to the computerisation of the society's business. At that time, the other leading societies were ahead of the Leek and Westbourne. There was a catching-up exercise to be done — an exercise so successfully undertaken that the Leek and Westbourne was to lead the movement in offering computerised accounting at the customer desks of its offices.

In 1966, Newton visited North America to absorb many of the latest ideas in the fast-growing world of computers. He looked at installations in Baltimore, Washington and Boston. Later that year, together with Cowburn, the general manager, and Webb, the chief accountant, Newton visited the London head offices of the Co-operative Permanent and Abbey National societies to study their computer costings.

In January 1968, the auditing and accounting firm, Price Waterhouse, was appointed as computer consultants. Their task was to carry out a feasibility study to find the best computer for the society's business and the best system of operation. Price Waterhouse had considerable experience in this kind of work, and particularly in competitive price ordering. A Leek and Westbourne computer steering committee was formed in April.

As a result of this exercise, it was decided in August to install a System 4-40 ICL computer for internal administration, processing the investment and mortgage accounts and providing statistical summaries. At that time, computers still relied on punched paper tape for their operation, a far cry from the sophistication of today's machines. The computer was intended for the new headquarters but in the meantime, temporary accommodation had to be found. The new computer department was first housed at No. 10 Stockwell Street where temporary rented accommodation was taken in November. But these premises — opposite New Stockwell House — soon proved too small and so St Luke's Church Hall, The Organ Ground, Leek, was taken on a twelve-month lease.

The financing of the computer also became a point of discussion among the board — whether to purchase outright or rent or lease. The decision in June the following year was to purchase.

This expansion of the Leek and Westbourne's activities was taking place against continuing uncertainty over the national economy. In March 1966, the Council of The Building Societies Association made it quite clear to the government that mortgage rates would have to rise again unless there was substantial relief in the Budget. But no relief was forthcoming and opinion in the movement hardened still further. In July, the upwards move came. Along with the other societies, the Leek and Westbourne raised its rate for new borrowers to 7⅛ per cent. Existing borrowers were to be given notice of an increase to the same level.

The government retaliated by calling in the Prices and Incomes Board to probe the Association's argument that the increase was necessary if building society activity were to be maintained and reserves not unduly reduced. Then came the seven-week seamen's strike of that year and a new economic crisis on top of the severe difficulties the Wilson administration was already facing. Bank Rate was raised to seven per cent, accompanied by a freezing of wages and dividends for six months and prices for twelve. This brought up the question of rates for existing mortgage borrowers and whether the Association could go ahead with its plans for raising them. In the circumstances, the Council decided to defer the recommended increase until 1st January, 1967. By December, worsening net receipts forced the Council to recommend that the share rate be increased at the same time to 4.25 per cent.

The Prices and Incomes Board reported before the December decision. Its finding was that there was no need for a rise in the mortgage rate in January if no change in the investment rate was required. This argument was rendered invalid by the December decision. But for the longer term, the Board queried whether societies needed the levels of reserves and liquidity ratio they operated. It recommended that a study be carried out by independent persons chosen jointly by the government and the Association. The result was that a committee of five was set up under the chairmanship of Mr Charles Hardie, a chartered accountant.

By May 1967, the government's deflationary measures appeared to be working and Bank Rate had come down to 5.5 per cent. By now too, there was a new Minister of Housing, Anthony Greenwood. His work was so to impress Newton, that he was invited in 1972, as Lord Greenwood of Rossendale, to join the board of the Leek and Westbourne. With the cut in Bank Rate, there was pressure on the building societies to reduce their rates, but they found much more of an ally in Greenwood than they had in his predecessor, Richard Crossman.

Greenwood made clear his position publicly. The "general view of The Building Societies Association is that to support a rising programme of house building the societies will have to retain their present investment and mortgage rates for the time being. My concern is that funds should be available for building private houses . . .". He was backed up by the Chancellor, James Callaghan, in October, who stated that "one difficulty that we have not been able to overcome is that your borrowing and lending rates are higher than you or I would like, but I fear that this is unavoidable at the present time. The world is going through a period of high interest rates and we are not exempt".

But the cut in Bank Rate was shortlived. By November, it had risen to eight per cent, following the crisis of the 1967 Middle East war and the devaluation of the pound from $2.80 to $2.40. Building societies found their flow of funds falling sharply.

Newton, at the Leek and Westbourne's annual luncheon in London in November, highlighted the dangers of the situation to the movement. If the eight per cent Bank Rate lasted for very long, more would have to be paid to investors and more charged for home loans. Building society interest rates could not remain below the general market level for any length of time.

"Societies will certainly not wish to see their present total savings eroded — and with it — substantial reductions in net current intake of funds, merely because high Bank Rate policy channels such funds to sources offering higher yields".

If, for example, the movement expanded lending by 15 per cent next year, the surplus for adding to reserves could well be below two per cent. "The result would be to reduce existing reserve ratios quite substantially".

The Hardie Committee reported in November. The existing requirements for trustee status specified the following totals: assets of

Transfer of Engagements. Silsden Building Society to Leek & Moorlands Building Society, 1959. Left to right, back row: J. Ainsworth (Leek), Col. Worthington (Leek), H. Leek (Leek), Sir Bernard White (Leek), W. Walker (Leek), M. Tatton (Leek), P. Taylor (Leek), Major Driver (Silsden), H. Ball (Leek), R. Todd (Leek), Hubert Newton (Leek), N. Cowburn (Leek). Seated: J. Bradley (Silsden), G. Tatton (Leek), H. Robinson (Silsden).

Transfer of Engagements. Stockport Atlas Building Society to Leek & Moorlands Building Society, 30th September, 1960. Left to right: A. Pickering (Stockport), D. M. Forsyth (Stockport), W. Walker (Leek), Hubert Newton (Leek), A. Brierley (Stockport), J. Guinan (Stockport), A. Hamer (Stockport), Col. Worthington (Leek), R. Todd (Leek), R. Rimmington (Stockport).

Transfer of Engagements. NALGO Building Society to Leek & Moorlands Building Society, 1st July, 1960. Left to right: Hubert Newton (Director & Secretary, Leek), G. H. Lees (Secretary, NALGO), A. D. Ogden (Director, NALGO), Sir Bernard White (Deputy Chairman, Leek), G. Watson Strother (Chairman, NALGO), S. R. Graydon (Director, NALGO), G. Tatton (Chairman, Leek), J. Ruscoe (Director, NALGO), W. C. Anderson (NALGO).

The former NALGO headquarters which housed the NALGO Building Society

not less than £500,000; reserves of 2.5 per cent for the first £100 million of assets, and two per cent for assets over £100 million; liquidity of not less than 7.5 per cent. These reserves were required to guard against losses on mortgages and losses on investment. The committee found that there was little real risk on either front. Mortgage losses since 1952 totalled just 0.011 per cent of total advances. As for investments, the regulations of the 1960 Act had effectively ended the purchase of long-dated securities, so removing any real danger from unwise investment.

The committee recommended a sliding scale beginning at 3.5 per cent on assets up to £500,000, and falling by stages to 1.5 per cent for assets between £100 million and £500 million. A flat rate of one per cent was proposed for assets above £1,000 million. Talks took place between the government and the Association and a revised scale was agreed both for the purposes of trustee status and membership of the Association. The percentages finally agreed were: up to £100 million of assets, 2.5 per cent; £100 million to £500 million, two per cent; £500 million to £1,000 million, 1.5 per cent; over £1,000 million, 1.25 per cent. The agreement of the building societies was reluctant, but the new scales were minimum ones. There was still freedom to adopt wider margins. On liquidity ratios, the Hardie Committee recommended that the 7.5 per cent figure be retained. This was agreed.

By March 1968, the situation of which Newton had warned had come about. Net receipts that month were just £22 million for the movement. There was now no question that both the investment rate and the mortgage rate must be increased. The Council recommended that from 1st May, 4.5 per cent be paid to investors and the mortgage rate be increased to 7⅝ per cent. The Leek and Westbourne brought in the rates but did not increase the mortgage rate for its existing borrowers. That rise did not take place until 1st January the following year.

Although the worst of the financial difficulties of the Labour Government were now over, interest rates generally remained high. To safeguard the movement's position against competing forms of saving, further increases were necessary in March 1969, the investment rate going up to five per cent and the mortgage rate to 8.5 per cent. The Leek and Westbourne again succeeded in keeping its mortgage rate for existing borrowers unchanged until 1st January, 1970.

One innovation by the Labour Government in the housing market was the mortgage option scheme. It came into effect on 1st April, 1968. It was aimed at those whose wages were too low to take full advantage of the tax relief on mortgages. Existing mortgage borrowers who wanted to opt into the scheme had been required to give notice by 31st December, 1967. Some four per cent of borrowers joined. They were charged a lower rate of interest but were precluded from all tax relief thereon. The difference was reimbursed to building societies by the government.

On the 1st April also, another government scheme started which was linked to the new option mortgage scheme. This second scheme enabled loans to be made by the societies of up to 100 per cent of valuation to those intending to take out new option mortgages. The advances were to be jointly guaranteed in each case by the government and an approved insurance company.

The trend to building society mergers was one which found favour with the Chief Registrar. In his report of 1969, he referred to the situation of the smaller societies in these terms: "For many the future can only hold stagnation. Directors should reflect upon the future, and, where there is no longer a worthwhile part to play, should ask whether it would not be better to merge with another society".

The Leek and Westbourne's formal takeover of the troubled Alliance Perpetual took place on 1st January, 1968. It coincided with another takeover — that of the Globe Building Society of Kingston-upon-Thames. The Globe had assets of £2,827,623. It had been founded in 1868. In November, the previous year, another London society, the Greater London Permanent Building Society of Farringdon Street, London, was taken over. In spite of its geographically-impressive name, it had assets of just £30,411. It dated back to 1903.

Two amalgamations much nearer to the Leek's old centre of activity took place later in 1968. In June, the Summit Building Society of Uttoxeter was taken over. It had been founded in 1964, and its assets totalled £115,820. In August, the Fenton Mutual Permanent Benefit Building Society of Stoke-on-Trent followed it into the Leek and Westbourne fold. The Fenton society had been founded in 1871 and its assets were £147,224. In August also, the Pembrokeshire Permanent Benefit Building Society of Pembroke Dock was taken over. It had assets of £696,803 and was founded just one year after the Leek and Moorlands — in 1857.

A third Staffordshire society was taken over a few months afterwards. The Town & Country Permanent Benefit Building Society of Burslem joined the Leek and Westbourne on 1st January, 1969. It dated back to 1869.

On the 1st April, 1969, the St Helens and Rainford Building Society, with assets of £1,274,208, came in. It had been founded in 1858. After this takeover, thereafter there was — in Leek and Westbourne terms — a comparatively long gap of eight months until 1st January, 1970, when the Stockport Victoria and Reddish Building Society was taken over. Its assets were £70,085 and it dated from 1962.

The last society to be taken over before the move to the new headquarters was the Keswick Benefit Building Society. Its assets of £842,923 were transferred on 1st March, 1970. It had been established in 1865.

An honour which delighted everyone at the society was a knighthood for Hubert Newton in the Queen's birthday honours list in June 1968. It was a fitting accolade for a man whose interests spanned the whole of the building society movement. He received the honour at Buckingham Palace in the company of his wife and daughter, Elisabeth.

Formal congratulations were given at a board meeting in Leek on 10th June. Brigadier Edwin Flavell, appointed deputy chairman the previous year, led the congratulations on behalf of his fellow directors. The general manager, Mr Norman Cowburn, congratulated Sir Hubert on behalf of the staff at the head and branch offices. A special event to mark the honour was held on 16th August in the form of a cocktail party at the rear of New Stockwell House. Some 220 members of the staff and their wives attended, and Brigadier and Mrs Flavell played host.

In July, Edward Moody retired from the Leek and Westbourne board. He was appointed at the same time to the London (West End board) which also comprised Mr Desmond Heap, solicitor and comptroller to the City of London, and Major G. L. Webb. The following year, on 14th April, Heap was recruited to the main board.

In February 1969, the society said goodbye to one of its longest-serving members, Mr John Hill, chief of the mortgage department, who had joined the Leek and Moorlands in 1934, just a year after Sir Hubert.

This was followed in August by an announcement that Sir Hubert himself was to stand down in September from the post of managing director. He was to continue as chairman. Although he formally relinquished executive powers, he was asked by the directors to continue in a consultative capacity. Sir Hubert's 64th birthday was in September, and he had now been with the society for 36 years. During that period, mergers had taken place with 31 other societies. The Leek and Westbourne itself was now the eighth largest in the country, with assets of over £250 million.

His successor was recruited from outside as Sir Hubert had been. Mr George Hardy, systems controller with the Co-operative Permanent, was appointed as chief general manager. He had not only extensive building society experience but had also spent some time in management consultancy. But he was to hold the post for less than a year before he resigned, and Mr Norman Cowburn, aged 50, the general manager, was appointed to it on 1st August, 1970. Like Sir Hubert, Cowburn had previously been with the Burnley Building Society, starting work there in 1936. He joined the Leek and Moorlands in 1954 as personal assistant to Sir Hubert.

Cowburn's move was accompanied by other changes at the top. Mr John Quipp was appointed general manager with responsibility for branches and agencies. Born and educated in Leek, he had joined the society in 1933 as a junior clerk. Leslie Beardmore and George Lees, the joint assistant general managers, were appointed deputy general managers. Beardmore had joined the Leek and Moorlands as a 14-year-old in 1926, becoming chief clerk in 1946, assistant secretary in 1959 and joint secretary in 1964. On 22nd July, Mr John Ainsworth, the previous deputy general manager, had retired, having been with the Leek and Moorlands since 1945.

In 1969, the formal arrangement of two joint head offices was ended, and New Stockwell House became the sole official headquarters, prior to the move. The Leek and Westbourne also resigned from the Metropolitan Association of Building Societies which it had joined at the time of the merger, and rejoined the Midland Association of Building Societies of which the Leek and Moorlands had been a member for most of its history.

The Leek and Westbourne also acquired new auditors. Its existing firm, Messrs Hudson Smith Briggs and Co decided to merge with the leading city firm of Price Waterhouse. Hudson Smith Briggs and Co had been appointed auditors to the Leek and Moorlands in 1895, their first year's fee being 30 guineas.

In October 1969, building societies were permitted by the government to join in the "save as you earn" contractual savings scheme, alongside the national savings movement. The Leek and Westbourne became an enthusiastic participant.

Another new type of investment was started by the society in January 1970, when it linked with the Liverpool-based Royal Insurance Group to offer a ten-year life assurance-linked savings bond. The scheme followed a number of other similar schemes between building societies and insurance companies. It offered one of the highest rates of return then available in the savings market — 13 per cent gross per annum to standard rate taxpayers up to the age of 30. It called for monthly savings between £5 and £50, with life cover 180 times the monthly premium. Dependent upon age, between 85 per cent and 95 per cent of each premium was invested with the Leek and Westbourne. The balance covered life assurance and administration. On survival to the end of the ten years, the bondholder received the total invested with the Leek and Westbourne, plus accumulated interest plus an amount equal to 2.5 times the monthly premium.

Sir Hubert described the Leek and Westbourne as a "reluctant debutante" in this market. But in a world where building societies were already taking the first tentative steps on the road to becoming financial conglomerates, the Leek and Westbourne felt it had no option but to make the facility available.

Although the formal opening of the new headquarters was not until October, the move into it started in May. In June, it acquired a name — Newton House. The staff were asked to submit their ideas for the name and "Newton House" came out top of the list. At the board meeting on 9th June, the directors unanimously agreed with the staff's choice.

The first phase of the move took place over the weekend of 16th/17th May when 170 staff were transferred from New Stockwell House, Milward Hall and St Luke's Church Hall. This left some 60 staff at New Stockwell House, and they were transferred in October.

The first board meeting at the new headquarters took place on 22nd June. Mr Roy Hewson, the deputy secretary, who had been seconded from his normal duties to oversee the project, was presented with a spode china bowl in appreciation. The registered office of the society was changed to Newton House from 1st June.

The official opening of Newton House took place on 21st October. Thirty-three years before, the town of Leek had come to a standstill as Sir Enoch Hill opened New Stockwell House. Now on the new spacious out-of-town site, a personality from a very different background, Sir Paul Chambers, a leading City figure and former chairman of ICI, opened the fourth headquarters of the society in Leek.

Some 260 people attended — directors and their wives, representatives of The Building Societies Association and of the Midland Association of Building Societies, directors and executives of fellow building societies, senior staff, businessmen with close links with the society, local councillors, architects, builders, and the press. A marquee was erected on the top car park for the luncheon following the opening.

Sir Paul unveiled a commemorative plaque at the entrance to Newton House.

A month later, on Saturday, 21st November, an open day was held for the public. About a thousand people took advantage of the invitation. A special booklet was published to commemorate the official opening, and the local weekly newspaper, the Leek Post and Times, published a twelve-page supplement to mark the open day.

In a foreword to the booklet, Sir Hubert stated his aims for the new headquarters: "Newton House is indicative of the age in which we live and has been designed for the challenge of the 70s which the Society is planning to meet with all its resources. I am greatly honoured that my name is associated with the building and, indeed, with the Society which I have served for some 37 years as its Chief Executive Officer.

"I joined the Society as Secretary in 1933 when total assets at that time were some £3,600,000. Today, we have reached some £290,000,000. I hope to see it reach £500,000,000 at least".

In fact, that figure was to be attained in just four years — helped along a little by the inflation of the early 1970s. By 1978, the society had £1,000 million in assets — far more than even Sir Hubert could have humanly anticipated in 1970.

The Leek Post and Times spoke of the development in these words: "The people of Leek are justly proud of their long association with the Building Society movement, and there is perhaps no more appropriate time than the present for them to consider the success of the Leek and Westbourne Society in particular.

"That success which has been enjoyed by the Society in recent years is out of all proportion to the size of the town in which it was born and in which it has retained its chief office ever since.

"Indeed the influence of the Society, and the name of Leek with it, has spread throughout all those parts of the world where Building Societies exist.

"Leek appreciates what the Society, and Sir Hubert Newton in particular, have done for the town. The Leek and Westbourne has not only provided employment and made a very considerable contribution to the local rate income but also — and perhaps most importantly — it has become a symbol of pride and confidence in the future of the town.

"Sir Hubert is not only the author of this Society's success story, but he is also one of the outstanding personalities in the international Building Society movement. His services to his Society, the whole movement, and his adopted town could be perpetuated in no better way than through the name of the Leek and Westbourne's magnificent new office".

Similar local sentiment was expressed in the supplement by the chairwoman of Leek Urban District Council, Mrs Joan Levitt: "Newton House will enhance employment opportunities in the town. It is a handsome building which does justice to the pleasant site which the locality was able to offer. All will hope that it has set a pattern for development which will convince other such enterprises that there is much to be said for situating them in a pleasant small town, not too far from a motorway, within easy access of magnificent countryside, and with no grave housing problems".

The building contained three sections — the main administrative office block, a small block on the north side housing the staff canteen, conference rooms and two flats for the caretaker and resident maintenance engineer, and a small link area incorporating the main staff entrance.

The site itself — on a sloping contour — was remodelled by the architects to make two main plateaux for the buildings. Trees were planted behind so that the parkland blended in with the adjacent Ballington Wood.

The main administrative block was built around a central courtyard for architectural effect and to let in natural light. The steel and concrete structure allowed for open spans of 40 feet, uninterrupted by any supporting pillars. This enabled an open plan office design to be used over much of the space. Open plan was also convenient for moving documents and materials about the building. But the open spaces were planned so that the areas were not too big. In the words of the architects: "In many respects, one large open space would have been ideal, but it was known that past experience indicated that this could be psychologically depressing for the staff working in the centre of such an area".

The building included a sub-basement built into the hillside. The basement accommodated a large store room for deeds and documents, a large garage and servicing area, stationery stores, paper storage facilities and plant rooms housing the boilers, refrigeration equipment, electrical plant, generators and air conditioning fans.

An impressive foyer fronted the building and the courtyard included an ornamental pool and fountain. The staircase from the foyer led up to the chairman's suite which incorporated the offices of the chairman and the chief general manager, the boardroom and secretarial offices.

The building was completely centrally heated and air-conditioned and was designed for a total of 350 staff.

It was visited by the architecture correspondent of the Financial Times, H. A. N. Brockman, who commented: "The design of the new building is simple and unaffected. As is so often the case in such circumstances, photography is not able to do it justice: its very simplicity lacks the large-scale boldness of texture the photographer likes so much".

He compared the new with the old: "While in this neighbourhood, I had the opportunity to see the previous headquarters building in Leek. This was designed by the architect Thorneley in the 'thirties: a very careful well-detailed traditional design with neo-classical overtones. While recognising the excellent materials and craftmanship and the soundness of his architectural competence, it was interesting to notice that, in spite of the present insistence upon more than good value for less money, Newton House has provided at the very least as good a result in today's difficult circumstances".

New Stockwell House remained in the society's ownership. It became the branch office of the Leek and Westbourne in the Leek town centre. The society assured the town that "full branch office facilities will always be available in the town centre for the convenience of members and others who wish to avail themselves of the facilities offered by the Society".

The Leek and Westbourne, eighth largest in the country in assets, was, in fact, fourth in the number of branch offices. At the time of the opening of Newton House, it boasted 106 branch offices and over 300 agencies throughout the United Kingdom. The biggest geographical concentrations were in the North Staffordshire/Cheshire/Shropshire areas, the North West of England, and London and the Home Counties. But branches were to be found as far afield as Belfast, Glasgow, Edinburgh and Hamilton, down to Wales and the South West of England.

For the Leek and Westbourne, the opening of Newton House meant security for the future. Whatever the pressures of expansion, the society now had not only a building which could cope but also a site which could cope. There was ample room for expansion in the new parkland setting.

The following year, 1971, saw the first annual meeting of the society to be held at Newton House — on 21st April. A year later, the old home of the Westbourne Park Building Society, Westbourne House, was sold and its staff moved to premises at 186 Queensway, London WC2. The mortgage deeds at Westbourne House were moved to Newton House.

So closed a chapter in which the Leek had found a London home, but then grew its roots even deeper in Staffordshire. It was a conscious decision. The opportunity had been there for the society to base itself permanently in London. But London held few of the advantages for a soundly-based national building society that it did for other banking and financial concerns. The Leek could run just as efficient an operation from its small town base, at less cost and with room for easy physical expansion. Modern communications and growing computer-isation were anyway making geographical position irrelevant.

9: The Leek, Westbourne and all stations to . . . .

THE BUILDING SOCIETY MOVEMENT was plunged in the early 1970s into a situation it had never encountered in its 200-year history — runaway house prices. The spiralling inflation posed problems for which past experience provided no guide. In the General Election of June 1970 the Conservatives under Mr Edward Heath won an unexpected victory. The new government was committed to make increased home ownership one of its major policy goals. Its purpose was to bring about a huge shift from the public rented sector and release financial resources weighing on the public purse. Council tenants were to be given the chance to own their own homes and subsidies to council housing cut down. Rents were to be steadily raised to "fair rent" levels.

The Conservatives wanted to raise sharply the level of owner-occupation from the then 52 per cent level, representing 17 million households. It was obviously a policy that the building societies welcomed. What they could not foresee was the financial chaos the new government's policy of lifting credit restrictions was ultimately to bring. Throughout the 1960s, house prices had risen at a steady pace. Soon they were to rise at an explosive pace.

The fear of rising unemployment lay behind the govenment's credit moves. In December 1970, the number out of work was under 600,000. By July 1971, it was 800,000, and had risen to 900,000 by January 1972. Reflationary measures during 1971 saw purchase tax cut by 20 per cent and hire purchase controls lifted. Bank Rate was cut to five per cent and long-established restrictions on bank competition lifted. Further tax cutting measures followed in the 1972 budget.

In this new climate of expansion, earnings rose rapidly, unhindered by the incomes policy the previous government had attempted. Average earnings rose by twelve per cent in 1970, eleven per cent in 1971 and thirteen per cent in 1972. The effect on house prices, historically at a low level in relation to earnings, began to show through dramatically. By the end of 1971, prices had gone up by 21 per cent. Between the end of 1971 and the end of 1973, they almost trebled. The word "gazumping" became a familiar term in the English language — defined as the practice whereby a seller having agreed one price then accepts a higher offer from someone else. Prices were rising so rapidly that many sellers were tempted into this practice.

The building society movement increased its lending from £1,950 million in 1970 to £2,705 million in 1971 and to £3,630 million in 1972. The figure for 1973 was £3,510 million. It remains a matter of lasting historical controversy whether building societies helped fuel the rise in house prices or were merely responding to the demand created by the Heath Government's credit expansion.

1972 saw pay restraint reintroduced and interest rates starting to rise again. Between the autumn of 1972 and the spring of 1973, there were to be four rises in the building societies' investment rate as rises in general interest rates gathered apace. The first came in October 1972. The Leek and Westbourne, in line with the rest of the movement, increased its share rate to 5.25 per cent and the rate on new mortgages to 8.5 per cent. In February 1973, the share rate went up again to 5.6 per cent. The Leek and Westbourne now applied the 8.5 per cent rate to its existing borrowers.

But Newton was beginning to get restless again. The issue was the familiar one. How far should the societies allow themselves to fall out of line with rates in other financial markets in the interest of national price stability? But the shock Newton applied to the system was greater than ever before.

The societies were now facing a record flood of withdrawals. In March The Building Societies Association decided to put off until the following month any decision on a higher mortgage rate, after talks with the government. It did recommend another increase in the share rate to 6.3 per cent.

The Leek and Westbourne now decided to break ranks. The 6.3 per cent rate was simply not high enough. Nor could the mortgage rate be held much longer. For Cowburn as chief executive, it was his first taste of being in the direct firing line with Sir Hubert. The Leek and Westbourne put its rate up to 6.5 per cent. And Cowburn put out a statement saying the society was thinking of putting the mortgage rate up to 9.65 per cent, a massive jump for those days of 1.15 per cent. Several smaller societies followed the Leek and Westbourne's initiative.

The move coming as it did amid the growing financial problems of the government attracted widespread comment. The economics correspondent of The Observer, Frances Cairncross, described the uproar in the movement and pointed out that the Leek decision had "upset many building society chiefs".

She continued: "It did not come as a surprise to some society chiefs for Sir Hubert Newton, chairman of the Leek and Westbourne, had told the last council meeting in no uncertain terms that he did not intend to abide by its recommendations. But some senior building society men are extremely cross. Mr Alan Mason, chief general manager of the Provincial, says: 'Competition is a good thing, provided that we are going to compete on equal terms'.

" . . . The critics point out that the borrower will almost certainly have to pay for the higher share rate. It is possible — though still not certain — that Leek's mortgage rate will go up to 9.65 per cent after next month's board meeting. 'This is most unfortunate', says Mr Roy Cox of the Alliance, 'at a time when the Government is having great difficulty in containing wage claims'.

"Sir Hubert Newton, ebullient chairman of Leek and Westbourne, certainly does not like high interest rates. 'They stink', he says succinctly. But he thinks that even at a rate of 9.65 per cent, a mortgage would still be a good buy. An ordinary borrower, paying tax at 30 per cent, would be paying interest at 6.755 per cent after tax relief. And to take the absurd position of someone paying tax at the top rate of 75 per cent, his interest would work out at 2.413 per cent. 'How silly', asks Sir Hubert, 'can you get?'

"Mr Norman Cowburn, Leek's chief general manager, says the higher rate for investors was necessary 'not to do the BSA in the eye, but because the withdrawal rate is the highest we've ever known. It has been mopping up virtually all new funds that come in'. Putting up the rate 'will be a very costly exercise, and it will definitely reduce the rate at which we can add to our reserves'.

"But Mr Cowburn defends the higher mortgage rate. Because of a quirk in the sliding scale for subsidies to option mortgage borrowers, a mortgage rate of 9.65 per cent will allow Leek to offer option borrowers a larger subsidy — three per cent — than a rate of 9.5 would have done. Leek at the moment has an unusually large number of option mortgage borrowers coming to it. 'That is the type of borrower we want to help', says Mr Cowburn".

The Leek and Westbourne's predicted mortgage figure worried the government considerably. The government feared the danger of mortgages soon going past the psychological ten per cent barrier. The result was a series of meetings between Ministers, Treasury officials and the Council of The Building Societies Association.

What transpired was an event hitherto unknown in building society history. The government offered to make an outright grant to the movement to prevent the rate going up to ten per cent. It proposed a grant for three months to make up the difference between an actual rate of 9.5 per cent and the ten per cent rate, at an estimated cost of £15 million.

This was a surprise for the societies who had not sought the grant at all or even envisaged a grant. The government's hope was that by the time the three months had passed, interest rates would be falling again. The Building Societies Association therefore recommended to members that the mortgage rate be raised to 9.5 per cent and the share rate to 6.75 per cent. The Leek and Westbourne, having played the crucial part in the crisis, agreed with the recommendation. Its 6.5 per cent rate lasted just through April before being increased to 6.75 per cent on 1st May. The 9.5 per cent rate was charged on new mortgages from the same date, and existing borrowers' rates were increased to 9.5 per cent from 1st July.

The Leek and Westbourne stated that it was considering not taking any of the government's money, but it relented and claimed £400,000 over the period concerned — 1st July to 30th September.

The half-yearly results of the Leek and Westbourne, announced in June, demonstrated clearly the difficulty the movement was having in maintaining lending levels. Only 7,450 mortgages were completed between January and June, compared with 10,500 in the corresponding period of the previous year. Actual advances totalled £42.2 million against £49.2 million. The value of loans awaiting completion at the end of the period fell by £6 million to £22 million.

The government's intended respite through its grant was only shortlived. The movement could not avoid the effects of the financial panic in other sectors of the economy. In a lull before the storm, in July, short-term interest rates were falling, and the Council of the Association thought it could return to a more stable situation. It decided to recommend a reduction in the share rate to 6.4 per cent and to keep the mortgage rate at 9.5 per cent when the government grant ran out. But the government's credit expansion policies started to go spectacularly wrong, with inflation accelerating and the balance of payments deteriorating fast. On the Friday after the Council's decision, the Minimum Lending Rate — the Bank of England base guide to interest rates at that time — was raised from 7.7 per cent to nine per cent. A week later, it jumped two per cent to eleven per cent. The Council had no option but to backtrack on its previous decision. The 6.75 per cent share rate was kept. The mortgage rate was raised to the dreaded ten per cent figure.

Still the situation was unstable. Bank deposit rates, local authorities' borrowing rates and other short-term rates had all gone up sharply because of the increase in Minimum Lending Rate. The joint stock banks were offering rates of up to 13 per cent for deposits — putting the building societies in an almost impossible competitive situation. The steep fall in receipts made it inevitable that rates would have to rise yet again in this amazing year. Even so, the government refused to bow to the inevitable. It persuaded the banks not to pay more than 9.5 per cent on deposits up to £10,000 in order to help the societies and avoid the mortgage rate increase.

The situation exacerbated Newton, who issued a public warning at the end of August that mortgage rates could rise to 14 per cent if the upward trend in interest rates was not reversed. Newton was one of the few leading building society figures who was not afraid to let his views be known publicly in the difficult political situation. But the newspaper reports of the time confirmed that others agreed with him although they would not say so. The situation was made even more difficult because the government was trying to enlist the help of the TUC in its anti-inflationary strategy. And the TUC leaders had already pointed out that one of their main concerns was the fear of a further rise in interest rates.

But the government's attempt at restraint was doomed to failure. Building societies could not ignore market conditions of so drastic a nature, as Newton pointed out. The mortgage rate was raised to a record eleven per cent and the share rate to 7.5 per cent. Even that record figure was a cautious increase bearing in mind Newton's reference to 14 per cent as valid in the conditions.

As with the other societies, the Leek and Westbourne was in a state of great activity as interest rates soared in the financial markets. A special general meeting of the board was called on 10th September to look at the situation four days before the Council of The Building Societies Association met. After the Council's decision to go for a record mortgage rate, the Leek and Westbourne board at their normal meeting on 24th September, agreed to bring in the new share rate from 1st October, and the record mortgage rate from the same date for new borrowers. Existing borrowers' rates were increased to the eleven per cent figure from 1st December.

Ironically, the Leek and Westbourne, which had gone through interest rate crises of a different kind under the past Labour government, went through this crisis with an ex-Labour minister as one of its directors. Newton had been very impressed with the performance of Anthony Greenwood as Minister of Housing. He persuaded his fellow directors to recruit Greenwood to the Board so the Leek and Westbourne could benefit as a leading society from Greenwood's political and housing expertise. Greenwood, now ennobled as Lord Greenwood of Rossendale, joined the board on 31st December, 1971. Edward W. Wallaker, from the society's London (West End) board, joined the main board at the same time. Greenwood had been a Member of Parliament from 1946 to the General Election of 1970, the year in which he was made a life peer.

The national economic crisis did not deter the Leek and Westbourne from steady expansion of its business nor from its declared merger policy which went on apace. There were also a number of other interesting events it had to cope with. The most important of these was the changeover of the national currency to decimal currency in February 1971. The operation was well planned in advance and went through smoothly. The new computer at Newton House was an invaluable aid. At the same time as the currency changeover, the society had to cope with the effects of a national postal strike which potentially could have had a more serious effect on it than on its more centrally-based rivals. Arrangements were made to pick up the mail from branches and agencies at various points throughout the country. There was some disruption to the society's operation but no long-term harm, thanks to careful planning.

On 29th June, 1971, another major accolade marked the contribution of Sir Hubert Newton to the building society movement. And it was in keeping with his deep-rooted attachment to Staffordshire. The University of Keele conferred on him the honorary degree of Master of Arts at a ceremony performed by the university's chancellor, Princess Margaret.

Following the postal strike at the start of 1971, another industrial emergency faced the Leek and Westbourne at the start of 1972, when a national state of emergency was declared because of power cuts. The society's standby electricity generator at Newton House was put into full use for the first time, and coped perfectly with no disruption to power and lighting.

In 1972 a staff association was formed at the Leek and Westbourne, following the passing of the Industrial Relations Act the previous year. The staff decided to form their own association rather than opt for membership of a national union.

An important innovation during the same year was an in-house printing operation which was to prove immensely useful in quickening up the society's responses to the ever-growing demands upon it. It was housed initially in New Stockwell House. In May 1973, a new ICL computer was installed at Newton House. The previous ICL 4/40 model was simply not powerful enough to cope with the volume of business. The new model was an ICL system 4/72 with much greater capacity.

An initiative by the Leek and Westbourne in the savings market came on 1st February 1973, with the introduction of a scheme for regular savers. It provided for regular savings to be made over a period of five years in shares, carrying an interest rate of seven per cent net of basic rate income tax.

On 1st July, 1973, Lord Greenwood performed the unveiling ceremony at Newton House of a portrait of Sir Hubert Newton by the artist Norman Hepple. The portrait hangs in the boardroom of Newton House.

The first merger after the move to Newton House came on 1st May, 1971, when the Leek and Westbourne acquired its first North Eastern society, the Wearside Building Society of Sunderland. The Wearside society had been founded in 1930 and had assets of £391,227. The merger gave the Leek and Westbourne a branch office in Sunderland.

Another Staffordshire merger came on 1st June when the Tunstall Building Society of Stoke-on-Trent was absorbed. It predated the Leek, having been set up in 1852. Assets were £2,337,950.

The merger came about because of a merger the Tunstall itself had undertaken a short time before — in September 1970 when it took over the Star Mutual Permanent Building Society of Burslem. After completing the merger, the Tunstall discovered discrepancies in the accounts of £250,000. This was a huge sum in comparison to its own total assets and so it sought the help of the Leek and Westbourne. The Leek and Westbourne, after taking over the Tunstall, began legal action to recover the money. The former chief cashier of the Star was found to be responsible and was sentenced to jail. The Leek and Westbourne's claim was eventually settled out of court for a gross payment of £132,500 in April 1977.

The 1st January, 1972, saw another two societies taken over, the New Homes Building Society of Twickenham in London, and the splendidly-named Queen Anne Building Society of Barnstaple in Devon. New Homes Building Society was started in 1958 and had assets of £1 million. The Queen Anne went back to 1868. Its assets totalled

Transfer of Engagements. Congleton Equitable Benefit Building Society to Leek & Moorlands Building Society, 1st October, 1961. Left to right: P. H. Taylor (Leek & Moorlands), A. Cropp-Hawkins (Congleton), Hubert Newton (Leek & Moorlands), Col. Worthington (Leek & Moorlands), V. Bloor (Congleton), H. Leek (Leek & Moorlands), J. Davis (Congleton).

Hubert Newton as President of the International Union of Building Societies and Savings and Loans Associations, accompanying HRH Princess Margaret when she opened its Congress at the Hilton Hotel, London, October 1965.

Sir Hubert and Lady Newton with their daughter Elisabeth after Sir Hubert had received his Knighthood, June 1968.

The Chairman and Managing Director Sir Hubert Newton and Lady Newton with the Board of Directors and Senior Executives at New Stockwell House, Leek, to mark the occasion of the Knighthood announced in the Birthday Honours List of HM Queen Elizabeth II, 8th June, 1968. Left to right: J. W. Yewdall (Secretary), H. Leek (Director), S. L. Masters (Deputy General Manager), J. Quipp (Branches & Agencies), S. Hill (Director), N. Cowburn (General Manager), Col. Worthington (Director), J. Webb (Chief Accountant), Brigadier Flavell (Deputy Chairman), E. Moody (Managing Director), Lady Newton, M. Nelson (Director), Sir Hubert, S. Green (Director) L. Beardmore (Assistant General Manager), P. H. Taylor (Director), J. C. Ainsworth (Deputy General Manager, M. Tatton (Director).

£1,806,155.

A lull in merger activity followed until 1st June, 1973, when the Paramount Building Society of Stafford followed its Tunstall county neighbour into the Leek and Westbourne fold. Its assets were £464,767. The society started in 1938.

But the lull was only the prelude to yet another massive merger. Talks went on throughout 1973 with the Ipswich-based Eastern Counties Building Society. The proposals were first disclosed on 21st June, 1973, with a target date of March 1974 for completion.

Like so many of the mergers of the Leek, it arose from Sir Hubert's wide contacts in the movement, contact which came easily to him because of his powerful and gregarious personality. Both Sir Hubert and the chairman of the Eastern Counties, Donald Gould, were past chairmen of The Building Societies Association and had known each other for many years.

The assets of the Eastern Counties totalled £42,568,364, making the total assets of the combined operation £530 million and putting it in seventh position in the assets table of building societies.

The June announcement said the merged society was to be called the Leek, Westbourne and Eastern Counties — an impossible mouthful of a name by any standards and which led to the playful designation in the building society movement of the "Leek, Westbourne and all stations to . . .".

The name change was agreed to at the annual general meeting of the Leek and Westbourne on 22nd April, 1974. A poll was held which resulted in 1,479 votes in favour and 29 against. The new name was to come into force from 1st May, the date settled on by the two societies for the formal merger of assets.

As with the Westbourne merger, Newton played a generous role in stepping down from the chairmanship so as not to over-emphasise the dominance of the bigger society's position. The chairmanship of the new board went to Lord Greenwood, Newton and Gould becoming deputy chairmen. The former head office of the Eastern Counties was to be called Ipswich Head Office. The chief office was to be Newton House. The merger provided branch offices at Bury St. Edmunds, Chelmsford, Colchester, Felixstowe, Stowmarket and Woodbridge. It was carried out without any staff reductions.

The main board of the united society contained all the directors in office at the time of the merger. It held its first meeting on Thursday, 7th May, 1974, at The Dorchester Hotel, London. The eight directors of the Eastern Counties society were elected to the board along with their fellow Leek and Westbourne directors. The board's composition was as follows:

Chairman, Lord Greenwood; Deputy Chairmen, Sir Hubert Newton and Mr Donald Gould; other directors, Brigadier Edwin Flavell, Mr S. S. Green, Sir Desmond Heap, Mr S. Hill, Mr W. M. Morfey, Mr M. A. Nelson, Mr G. W. Pipe, Mr M. J. Slater, Mr L. A. E. Stevens, the Hon. P. A. Strutt, Mr P. H. Taylor, Mr E. W. Wallaker, Mr H. A. Warner, and Mr R. H. Willett.

Sir Clavering Fison, previously Life President of the Eastern Counties, was appointed to the office of Honorary Life President. Two regional boards were formed — the East Anglian and the North Staffordshire.

The East Anglian board was: Chairman, Mr Gould; other directors, Messrs Pipe, Morfey, Slater, Stevens, Warner, Willett, The Hon. P. A. Strutt, and Mr F. J. Sharman. The North Staffordshire board was: Chairman, Sir Hubert Newton; other directors, Lord Greenwood, Brigadier Flavell, Sir Desmond Heap, Messrs Green, Hill, Taylor, Nelson, Wallaker, and Mr Norman Cowburn, who became Chief General Manager of the combined societies.

The Joint General Managers were Mr John Quipp (based at Leek) and Mr F. J. Sharman (Ipswich). Deputy General managers were Mr George Lees (London/NALGO), Mr F. M. Shaw (Ipswich) and Mr T. C. Mackay (Leek). Chief Accountant was Mr J. W. Webb and the Assistant General Manager, Mr T. C. Lyne. The secretary was Mr J. W. Yewdall.

Gould, the joint chairman, had served as chairman of The Building Societies Association from 1963 to 1965, the time of Sir Hubert's presidency of the International Union. Now 69, he had started his career with the Ipswich Permanent society, joining the Eastern Counties in 1929, some eight years later. He had also been a well-known sportsman in the area, playing soccer for Felixstowe and captaining the Ipswich and East Suffolk Cricket Club.

The merger did not prove to be the complete amalgamation that the Leek and Moorlands/Westbourne Park was. Even today, the Ipswich head office remains with some degree of separate organisation from Newton House. The reason essentially lay in the geographical differences of the Westbourne Park and the Eastern Counties. The Westbourne was one of a number of large London societies. With the selling of its old headquarters in April, 1972, and the movement of its mortgage deeds to Newton House, the connection with its previous independent history was severed. The Eastern Counties, in contrast, was a strong regional society, very much as the Leek and Moorlands had been in the past. Its Ipswich base and its prominence in East Anglia ensured that its organisation would keep much of its separate identity.

The Eastern Counties Building Society was, in fact, an older society than the Leek — by just one year. Its first title was something of a mouthful even by Victorian standards — The Eastern Counties Permanent Benefit Building Copyhold Enfranchisement and Investment Society. The name was not changed until almost half a century later when the society became the Eastern Counties Permanent Benefit Building Society in 1904. It was not until January, 1938, that the name became simply Eastern Counties Building Society.

The first board meeting is recorded as having taken place at Mr Pearce's Rooms, Princess Street, Ipswich, on Friday, 10th August, 1855, at half-past seven in the evening. Originally, there were two trustees, nine directors, two managers, two auditors, a solicitor and a consulting actuary. The original board of directors comprised Messrs S. Abbott, H. G. Bristo, J. Collins, I. Frost, S. Hayward, E. Hopson, J. Hunt, O. B. Lucas, and W. Green.

The balance sheet of October 1879, recorded the address of the society as No. 4 Princess Street, Ipswich. In 1922, the society built an office on a site in Museum Street, Ipswich (later called No. 40), having purchased the land for £750. The builders were Messrs Cubitt and Gott, and the cost of construction was £2,555. The architect, Mr John Corder, was a director of the society.

It found that continued growth made even the new premises inadequate. Eight years later, the society bought a building at 13 Queen Street, Ipswich, which it moved into on Saturday, 26th July, 1930, after carrying out extensive alterations. In 1937, the adjacent building of 15 Queen Street was bought for £3,500.

The first joint managers of the society were Mr John Clarke and Mr Joseph Pearce. Clarke only held office for a short time but Pearce remained until 1877 when he was succeeded by his son, Mr Arthur Pearce. The Pearces established something of a family dynasty in the Eastern Counties for when Arthur Pearce died in 1915, his son Mr Arthur James Pearce became the manager. On the death of Arthur James Pearce in 1921, Mr Harry Foyster, who had been secretary since 1915, was appointed manager and secretary, an office he held until retirement on 31st October, 1946. Donald Gould took over the combined posts until 1962 when he was appointed to the new post of managing director. Mr John Sharman took over as secretary. Gould became chairman in 1967, retaining his post of managing director.

Whereas the Leek and Moorlands' early records show much lending to local silk, pottery and textile works, the Eastern Counties' early records have a different, East Anglian flavour. They show advances made on windmills, which were considered good business securities.

The Eastern Counties had been in takeover activity of its own before the merger with the Leek and Westbourne. It strengthened its dominant position in Ipswich in 1967 when it took over the Ipswich Permanent Benefit Building Society on 1st September. Mr Wallace Morfey, who came onto the Leek, Westbourne and Eastern Counties board, had been a director of the Ipswich Permanent since 1951. Mr Ronald Willett, who also came onto the board, had been a director of the Ipswich Permanent since 1959.

The first policy decision to face the Leek, Westbourne and Eastern Counties board was whether to take advantage of yet another offer of state funds — this time from the Labour Government under Harold Wilson, which had succeeded the Heath Government in February, 1974.

One of the last initiatives of the Heath Government in housing finance had been an attempt to set up a more stable flow of money to housebuyers. The idea had been mooted of a stabilisation fund but the government — much to the relief of the societies — fended off this idea and decided instead to set up a so-called Joint Advisory Committee, consisting of representatives of the Department of the Environment, the Treasury, the Bank of England, the Chief Registrar's Office and the Council of The Building Societies Association.

Among its objectives was a flow of mortgage funds sufficient to enable the housebuilding industry to plan for a high and stable level of housing for sale. An order of mortgage preference was laid down with first-time purchasers put at the head of the mortgage priority list. Buyers of new dwellings were given the second priority place.

The committee's aim was to study all aspects of the housing market and to forecast the level of investment receipts needed to achieve housing targets.

It was set up in October, 1973, just before the Arab-Israeli war broke out. The resulting surge in oil prices plus severe industrial trouble at home soon led to more crisis measures by the Heath Government. Severe limits on credit and public spending were introduced and Minimum Lending Rate raised to 13 per cent in November. Industry went on a three-day week in January, 1974.

The building societies faced another disastrous situation with net receipts plummeting and actually changing to an outflow of £15 million in February, 1974. Competitive savings offers did not help. Local authority yearling bonds carried a 14.5 per cent of rate of interest and guaranteed income bonds 12.5 per cent.

The role of the Joint Advisory Committee now changed to a line of contact between the building societies and the new Labour Government which came to power in the wake of the crisis. The new government decided not on an outright grant to the societies to hold down the mortgage rate but instead to lend them £100 million during April at a rate of 10.5 per cent and to make a further £400 million available, if needed, in the next four months, The loans were conditional on societies not increasing their interest rates to investors or borrowers.

Under the scheme, the Leek and Westbourne — then in its last days of existence — would have been entitled to £2,952,000 of the first £100 million. But the prospect was more than Newton and his board could bear. Newton had been extremely wary of the previous outright grant, This latest scheme, he felt, could prove the wedge for direct state involvement in the building society movement. So the Leek and Westbourne announced publicly through a press statement that it would not be taking the money. It pointed to the strength of its own position. The inflow of investment money had improved and its current liquidity position was very healthy. The Leek, Westbourne and Eastern Counties on its formation had to decide whether to accept the further allocations to which it was entitled. It continued the Leek and Westbourne policy of shunning the offer.

In July, the society launched another investment initiative — the term bond which offered investors a higher rate of interest in return for their agreeing to tie up their money with the society for a fixed period. This was a logical response to the increasing volatility of building society funds. The idea had first been introduced in the 1960s but had not been popular then. In those days of more stable rates, it was seen as an unwelcome inducement to investors to switch funds.

The Leek, Westbourne and Eastern Counties term bonds were offered for fixed periods to twelve months and two years, thereafter subject to withdrawal at three months' notice. The rate of interest on the twelve months' bonds was to be 1.5 per cent above the share rate, and on the two year bonds, 1.25 per cent above. Interest was to be paid half-yearly. At the same time, the directors increased the rate of interest on the Regular Monthly Savings Shares to 8.75 per cent. On 1st August, the interest rate on the two year bonds was reduced to 8.5 per cent from 8.75 per cent.

Soon after its formation, the Leek, Westbourne and Eastern Counties suffered the sad and sudden death of its chief accountant, John Webb. His successor was Michael Shaw, Deputy General Manager (East Anglia). He had joined the Eastern Counties in 1967 as chief accountant and had held the post until the merger.

In May, 1975, Sir Hubert Newton ended his 35-year membership of the Council of The Building Societies Association. He was its longest serving member and had reached the age limit for membership, Norman Cowburn took his place and was also elected chairman of the Midland Association of Building Societies for 1975/76.

The Leek, Westbourne and Eastern Counties did not take long to hit the takeover trail again, in spite of the obvious problems of bringing its own organisation together. On 1st July, 1974, the Oldbury Britannia Building Society in the West Midlands was absorbed. It had been founded in 1909 and had assets of £1,135,659. On 1st January, 1975, another North Eastern society came into the fold in the form of the Consett Reliance Building Society. It dated back to 1906 and its assets were £841,047. On 31st March, the City of Cardiff Permanent Building Society was absorbed, It assets were £4,696,107 and it dated also from 1906.

The Oldbury takeover was obviously a takeover of a minnow by a giant. But it could humorously be said that the Oldbury took over the Leek, Westbourne and Eastern Counties. For it was to rid that society of its cumbersome name and give to it its own splendid title — Britannia.

It had been obvious to Newton and the board for some time that a new name was needed. The Oldbury merger put the idea of Britannia in Newton's head. It had exactly the right tone for a national society of the Leek, Westbourne and Eastern Counties' standing. At that time, the building society movement was examining how it could make use of Britain's membership of the Common Market following entry in 1973. Britannia was a name which would immediately have impact if and when the British societies were permitted to expand into Western Europe.

A special resolution to change the society's name was put forward by the board at the annual meeting at Newton House, on 24th April, 1975. The move aroused deep feelings. The "Leek" name had been in continuous use since 1856 and it was a proud one. No longer would the name of the town be represented in the title of one of the major building societies in the country. Nine members questioned the need for change and a poll was taken. It showed 3,101 for the change and 695 against.

The change of the name was to come into effect from 28th December, 1975. The Leek, Westbourne and all stations to . . . had found its final station.

10: Rule Britannia

CHANGING THE NAME of the society so completely, obviously carried a risk. As in other fields of business, brand names carry loyalty with them and a feeling of identity for the customer. A new name could damage this continuity and so hurt the steady progress of the past years. Although the Co-operative Permanent had successfully changed its name to the Nationwide in 1970, the conventional wisdom in the building society movement was that name changes were a costly and unnecessary business.

A massive advertising campaign was launched to promote the new name. Some £200,000 of media advertising was commissioned from the Haddons agency for the ten days following the name change. A total of £500,000 spending was planned by Haddons for the next two years. An initial £100,000 Project Britannia campaign had already been carried out the previous July as a preparatory step to the relaunch.

The ten days of immediate advertising concentrated on stating the change of name. The following two years of advertising were to make a general appeal to the investor, particularly to the lower socio-economic groups which the movement was trying to draw in. The Project Britannia campaign had used the slogan "Britannia helps your money fight back." That was kept for the general advertising campaign.

In many ways, the society was retreading the ground it had trod at the time of the merger with the Eastern Counties. Then in a series of advertisements, it had used the slogan the "Leek and who?" Having successfully brought to national attention the Leek, Westbourne and Eastern Counties name, it was now having to undo its work.

Although 1975 was a time of hectic planning for the changeover, the nascent Britannia did not let up its activity on other fronts. Between the time of the decision to change the name and the changeover on 28th December, 1975, two more societies were absorbed. On 1st July, the Bath Liberal Building Society was absorbed. It was founded in 1869 and had assets of £3,455,659. The society was especially interesting historically as one of the few formed to promote a political interest, although the Liberal Party connection had long since disappeared. An extract from its first minute book reads:

"It having been considered advantageous that a Building Society should be established in this City under the auspices of the Liberal Party with a view of enabling the Working Men to secure for themselves a Dwelling House by means of small savings; a few friends met together from time to time to mature the plan of such a Society and having obtained the names of parties willing to take upwards of 100 Shares, a meeting of those whose names were subscribed as intending Shareholders was held at No 3 Paragon on Wednesday, the 8th of September (1869) for the purpose of electing officers and of carrying into effect the instructions of those who desired the formation of a Society as described."

The minute book records that Mr R. P. Edwards was appointed chairman and Messrs Jerom Murch, James Chaffin, and W. C. Jolly as trustees. Out of three names submitted, a Mr Moore was appointed secretary. A ballot was held for the election of directors and Messrs T. D. Archard, W. F. Downes, Solomon Francis, William Flower, Alfred Jones, S. W. Knight, William Lewis, and Alfred Taylor were chosen.

The minutes continued: "Various suggestions having been made and having taken into consideration that our opponents had distinguished their Society by the term Conservative, it was resolved that its title should be 'The Bath Liberal Permanent Mutual Benefit Building Society'." The balance in the bankers' hands at the end of 1869 was shown as £35.10s.0d.

On 1st November, 1975, the Chesterfield Benefit Building Society was absorbed into Britannia. It was founded in 1855 and had assets of £456,532.

At its annual meeting on 24th April, 1975, the Leek, Westbourne and Eastern Counties lost two of its former Eastern Counties directors through the retirement of Mr M. J. Slater and Mr L. A. E. Stevens. At the September board meeting, a new organisational structure was decided on. Henceforth, a new "Executive Committee" would meet each month, with the main board meeting six times a year.

The first Executive Committee meeting took place on 18th November but the idea did not prove a success and the committee was wound up in June 1976.

In the same month as the annual meeting, the government took the step of restricting lending for house purchase by local authorities. This decision formed part of a programme cutting back on public spending. The building societies were asked to help fill the gap by setting aside £100 million for loans to would-be buyers passed over to them by the local authorities. These were buyers who usually sought an advance on an older property.

The scheme was administered on a regional basis, and the society agreed to be involved in four areas — Eastern, North West, East Midlands and West Midlands.

Another joint investment initiative with the Royal Insurance company came in November. Under it, so-called "annuity mortgages" were provided for older people, particularly pensioners.

On 24th November, leading personnel from the society attended a reception and supper at the Guildhall in the City of London, organised by The Building Societies Association to commemorate the 200th anniversary of the founding of the first-known building society, Ketley's of Birmingham. The Queen and the Duke of Edinburgh were present.

The constant expansion of the society meant continuing accommodation problems even with the benefits Newton House brought. During 1975, premises were bought in Strangman Street, Leek, to house the printing department and stationery store which had outgrown their accommodation at New Stockwell House. The following year, a staff sports and social club was set up on the first floor of the Strangman Street premises. The club was opened on 5th October by Sir Hubert Newton and Norman Cowburn.

Less successful was a major property project in London. For some time, the board had been considering buying premises in Cannon Street, London, to set up a City branch office. The expected purchase price was £5 million, to which had to be added another £2 million for modernisation and refurbishing both for the society's needs and to make the vacant parts attractive for outside letting. The costs and the difficulties of altering the premises led the board to withdraw from the scheme in March 1976. Later that year, an imposing new office was opened on Euston Road, when the NALGO trade union moved to a new headquarters building on the corner of Euston Road and Mabledon Place.

It was in 1976 that the sad decision was made to sell the society's former headquarters at New Stockwell House, Leek. But the purchasers were Staffordshire Moorlands District Council, so the building's proud tradition of public service was continued.

On 1st September, 1976, a new Ipswich head office was opened by Donald Gould — Queen's House. A month after the opening — on 4th October — Britannia said goodbye to one of the stalwarts of the Eastern Counties Building Society, Mr John Sharman, who retired as General

Manager (East Anglia) after completing 50 years of service. Mr Philip Lay was appointed to succeed him, taking on the title of Ipswich Head Office Manager.

At the end of November, Lord Greenwood stepped down from the chairmanship although he retained his seat on the board. Sir Hubert Newton now became chairman of Britannia with Donald Gould as deputy. Lord Greenwood in a press statement said he wanted to be able to devote more time to his other work on national housing issues, particularly to his work in the voluntary housing movement. Twice before, Sir Hubert had stepped down from the chairmanship. Now he was to resume once again the formal leadership to which he was so richly entitled.

By 1976, national economic troubles were again reasserting themselves after two good years for the movement which saw plentiful receipts, the share rate falling to 6.5 per cent and the mortgage rate to 10.5 per cent.

The economic problems faced by the Labour Government saw interest rates changed eight times between April 1976 and November 1978. The building society movement had learned a severe lesson from the times of the Heath Government. Now as interest rates went up and down, they followed closely so that market conditions did not catch them out.

In 1976, the Labour Government agreed with The Building Societies Association on guidelines for restrictions on mortgage lending. Total lending was to be kept to or under £510 million a month. Another restriction agreement followed in 1978 with the movement limiting itself to £720 million a month for the first six months of the year.

Part of the reason for the restriction was the strong criticism from the banks of the increasing share of the nation's savings being absorbed by the building societies. Between 1966 and 1977, the building societies' share of personal sector short term assets had gone up from 24 per cent to 43 per cent. The societies countered this argument by pointing out that much of the money was recycled money as first-time buyers in the pre-war period died and left the asset value of their houses to their children. Whatever the pros and cons of this complex argument, the societies went along with the government in the hope—a successful hope as it turned out—of keeping up a stable inflow of funds and outflow of mortgage money in contrast to the disruption of the early 1970s.

The £720 million figure was cut to £610 million after just three months because the government felt that the levels of mortgage lending were forcing up house prices. Britannia's allocation on this basis was

£17.18 million a month. The rate was increased to £640 million a month from July to December, and the Britannia's figure increased in proportion.

The interest rate changes saw Britannia cut its share rate and mortgage rate by 0.5 per cent on 1st June, 1976, to 6.5 per cent and 10.5 per cent respectively. In October, the Council of The Building Societies Association was actually discussing by how much it should raise rates when the news came through to the meeting that a record Minimum Lending Rate of 15 per cent had been announced. The meeting then made a recommendation that a record mortgage rate of 12.25 per cent be brought in and a record share rate of 7.8 per cent. Britannia brought in the new share rate from 1st November and the higher mortgage rate from the same date for new borrowers. Existing borrowers had a respite until 1st December before suffering the increase.

From 1st May, 1977, the share rate was reduced to seven per cent against a background of falling interest rates generally. The mortgage rate came down to 11.25 per cent.

At the same time, the board made an important change of policy on mortgage rates for new borrowers. It introduced a scale of differential mortgage rates on new mortgages above £15,000. The rates came into effect on 26th April, and were: £15,000-£17,500, 11.5 per cent; £17,501-£20,000, 11.75 per cent; £20,001-£22,500, 12 per cent; £22,501-£25,000, 12.25 per cent. The rates for sums over £25,000 were to be by special arrangement.

By this time, the society had a large range of rates of interest, because of the development of special and regular savings schemes. The complexity of rates on the mortgage side was added to by the growth of endowment mortgages in addition to the option scheme mortgages. Endowment mortgages carried a slightly higher rate of interest than the normal mortgage — at this time about 0.25 per cent.

In August, the share rate dropped again to 6.7 per cent and other savings rates fell in line. The basic mortgage rate dropped to 10.5 per cent for all existing and new mortgages, the differential level being scrapped.

Rates tumbled again in the autumn, down to a six per cent share rate for new investors from the 1st November, and from 1st January the following year for existing investors. The basic mortgage rate dropped to 9.5 per cent for new borrowers from 24th September and for existing borrowers from 1st October, but the differential scale was reintroduced with a top figure of 10.5 per cent on mortgages from £22,501 to £25,000 and specially negotiated rates above £25,000. A differential scale was also introduced for endowment and option scheme mortgages.

1978 saw a fall on 1st February to 5.5 per cent in the general share rate with corresponding falls in the other savings rates. The mortgage rate was reduced to 8.5 per cent on the normal basic mortgage from 14th January for new borrowers and from 1st February for existing borrowers, with other rates being changed accordingly.

The fall was shortlived and rates went up again in the summer. The share rate went up to 6.7 per cent from 1st July. The normal basic mortgage rate went up to 9.75 per cent for new borrowers from 13th June and for existing borrowers from 1st August.

In the winter came yet another in the long and continuous line of changes. The general share rate went up to eight per cent and the normal mortgage rate to 11.75 per cent for new borrowers from 14th November and for existing borrowers from 1st January, 1979.

These continuous changes — a result of the government's international monetary crisis — would have amazed the society's forbears. They had been used to decades of stable rates. Now rates changed and changed again in just months. Computerisation was the key to the successful running of the society during all this upheaval. Without computerisation, there could have easily been chaos.

1977 saw a change in the executive structure of Britannia. Norman Cowburn, the Chief General Manager, now took the title of Managing Director and became a member of the board of directors. Mr John Quipp, the General Manager, became Deputy Managing Director. Mr Michael Shaw, the Chief Accountant, became General Manager, and Mr John Yewdall, the Secretary, was appointed Deputy General Manager and Secretary. Mr Travis Lyne, the Assistant General Manager, and Mr Roy Hewson, Staff Officer, were appointed Deputy General Managers. Mr Barrie Dolphin was appointed Assistant General Manager.

The restructuring took place at the end of April. At the same time, Brigadier Flavell and Mr Nelson retired from the board. Both had been directors of the old Westbourne Park society before the merger.

April also marked the launch of the society's staff magazine, *Roundabout*. This was to a large extent made possible by the steady growth of the society's in-house printing operation which produced the magazine. *Roundabout* was to be published quarterly.

Britannia now made an important policy decision — to boost its lending in inner city areas by going into a pilot scheme with Birmingham City Council. This followed attention drawn to the problem of inner city areas in a Green Paper, called the Housing Survey, published in 1977.

Against the background of frequently changing interest rates, Britannia still found time to innovate in its investor packages. From 1st June, 1978, it introduced a "Double Investment" plan, which again involved a link-up with the Royal Insurance group. Investors were able to make a lump sum investment with Britannia out of which an insurance premium was paid to the Royal for an endowment policy. The policies were fixed ten-year endowments, and, on the assumption that the investment account remained open for the full ten years, it was intended to pay a bonus at the end of the ten years amounting to three per cent of the initial investment. At the same time, the board approved a cut in the minimum investment for term shares from £1,000 to £500.

This was followed in September by the introduction of a new five-year bond, the Britannia Escalator Bond. This was planned to have an interest differential above the general share rate, increasing each year.

The 1970s had produced a whole array of new investment terms in the building societies, and the managerial task of looking after the range of policies and seeing that adequate returns were produced, was a considerable one. Certainly, building societies had become far more complex institutions. It was the use of computers which enabled these new policies to be issued so efficiently and smoothly.

The merger policy went on apace. Two Wiltshire societies came into the Britannia family in 1977 — the Calne and District Permanent Benefit Building Society and the Westbury and District Permanent Building Society. The Calne and District came in on 1st October. It had assets of £850,000 and had been founded in 1886. The Westbury and District came in on 1st November. It had assets of £1,350,000 and had been founded in 1907.

On 1st April 1978, the Glantawe Permanent Benefit Building Society of Swansea was absorbed. It had been founded in 1906 and its assets were £4 million.

The building society movement was shaken by two scandals in the late 1970s. Once again, laws and regulations which were thought to provide total security were found to be sadly wanting.

The first involved the Wakefield Building Society of Wakefield in Yorkshire, a society hitherto regarded as one of unblemished respectability. An audit by newly appointed auditors in 1976 discovered widespread deficiencies in the society's books, amounting to at least £600,000. The manager of the society was a Mr William Robinson who had held the post since 1949 and had been a director since 1954. He was nearing 70 in 1974 when the society appointed a new general manager-designate who was professionally qualified as a chartered secretary and had served with two other societies. He became suspicious about the society's book keeping, and in 1976 the new auditors were brought in. Robinson subsequently confessed to keeping fictitious accounts and to using the money so gained for his own purposes. He was later jailed for six years and a criminal bankruptcy order was made against him. The society was taken over by the Halifax Building Society in October, 1976.

This was followed in 1978 by a far bigger scandal and probably the most bizarre ever witnessed in the building society movement. It involved the Grays Building Society of Grays in Essex. Like Robinson, the man at the centre of the Grays scandal had exercised total personal domination over the society for many years. He was Harold Percy Jaggard, secretary of the society since 1927, secretary and director since 1963, and secretary and chairman since 1974.

Jaggard had for over 40 years systematically defrauded the Grays society. The fraud was discovered in March 1978 and it amounted to the staggering sum of £7 million out of supposed assets of £11 million. Of the £7 million total, £2 million was direct theft by Jaggard and £5 million represented the lost interest to the society over the many years the fraud had been perpetuated. Jaggard committed suicide the day the fraud was discovered. He was later found to have spent about £1.6 million on gambling on horse and dog racing.

The fraud posed the building society movement with an enormous problem. Should they simply leave the Grays investors to their fate — the liquidation of their society and most of their money lost. Or should they launch a rescue fund, an idea from which they had shied away in past and much more minor scandals. For the good of the movement, The Building Societies Association decided along with the Chief Registrar that a rescue fund was the inevitable course of action. The power to do this under the Building Societies Act, 1962, had first to be tested in the courts. The case was heard by Mr Justice Templeman in May 1978, and judgment was given in favour of the rescue scheme. Britannia's contribution to the compensation fund came to £228,000. Total contributions came to a figure of 0.0235 per cent of the movement's total assets. The Grays business was taken over by the Woolwich Equitable.

The Chief Registrar of Friendly Societies reminded societies that under the 1962 Act, it was the responsibility of directors to ensure that proper books of account were kept and that a proper system of supervision of cash and receipts was operated. Two inspectors were appointed by the Chief Registrar to investigate the Grays fraud and they reported in May 1979, with trenchant criticism of the laxity which led to the scandal.

In the aftermath, Britannia agreed in 1979 to support a voluntary Investors' Protection Scheme arranged by The Building Societies Association.

In 1975 and 1976, Britannia had briefly experimented with the idea of an executive committee in addition to the main board. A similar idea was launched in August 1978, with the formation of a General Purposes Committee to examine issues of major importance which the board felt it could not deal with adequately in the time available at its monthly meetings.

The new committee consisted of the chairman, deputy chairman, managing director, deputy managing director and board members Taylor, Wallaker and Willett. It was given the power to co-opt at any time any other member of the board with relevant specialised knowledge, and to call on any of the other executives or departmental heads for information.

In September 1978, a new coat of arms was approved for Britannia. The arms were designed by H. Ellis Tomlinson, Heraldic Adviser to The Building Societies Association. On the shield, against a blue sky, the society's emblem, Britannia, patrols the red and white battlemented walls of the Englishman's home. On the crest is depicted a grassy mound denoting land ownership. A black portcullis stands on the mound with gold nails and chains attached to two gold keys, symbols of security, trusteeship and home ownership. These symbols, together with the gold "Eastern Crown" topping the portcullis, come from the arms of the Eastern Counties Building Society. The supporters are red lions collared with gold Staffordshire knots, both originating in the Staffordshire county arms, and, with the brick-axes, derived from the former arms of the Leek society. The motto is "With Britannia on guard, the home is safe — Custode Britannia Domus Tuta".

A milestone in the history of the society was passed in April 1978, when the asset figure of £1,000 million was reached. To mark the event, a special supplement was produced in the Leek Post and Times.

The paper commented: "Britannia Building Society's one-billion-pound achievement is an admirable milestone not only for the society itself, but for the town of Leek.

"For 122 years there has been a happy partnership between the

The former Eastern Counties Building Society

The Directors and Chief Executives in the new Board Room at Newton House, 1970. Left to right: J. W. Yewdall (Secretary), G. H. Lees (Assistant General Manager), J. Quipp (General Manager), N. Cowburn (Chief General Manager), Directors, M. A. Nelson, S. Hill, M. A. Tatton, H. Leek, Sir Hubert Newton (Chairman), Brig. E. W. C. Flavell (Deputy Chairman), Lt. Col. G. J. Worthington, P. H. Taylor, S. S. Green, Sir Desmond Heap, L. Beardmore (Deputy General Manager), S. L. Masters (Deputy General Manager), J. C. Chaplin (Secretary).

Honorary Life President
1974-1985
Sir Clavering Fison, DL,
Chairman of the Eastern Counties
Board from 1944-1966,
Honorary Life President, Eastern
Counties 1966-74.

Donald Gould, FCBSI
Former Chairman and Managing
Director, Eastern Counties
Building Society.
Director, Eastern Counties
Society 1962-1974.
Director, Britannia Building
Society 1974-1980.
Deputy Chairman, Britannia Building
Society 1974-1979.

moorland community and the organisation that has grown to become one of the country's top ten building societies. Although 'Leek' is no longer in the name, Britannia knows its name is here.

"By providing the money to buy a house, the society has played a very important part in the lives of countless thousands of local folk, and to many more Britannia means a safe — and rewarding — place to keep the family funds.

"But the mutual benefits go much further. Britannia is a major local employer, providing good conditions, good pay and good social facilities to 350 people in the Leek area. The society's relations with its workers is a fine example to the rest of local commerce: Newton House is the very model of a modern, clean and pleasant working environment — and so are the branch offices".

Sir Hubert in a foreword to the supplement pointed out Britannia's position as ninth largest society in the country and its claim now to be among the billionaires of building societies.

Britannia now accounted for 155 branches, 1,200 staff and 650,000 investors across the United Kingdom — from Inverness in the north of Scotland to Camborne in the south west of England.

To deal with this wide geographical spread, the society divided its branches between nine regions: Scotland and Northern Ireland; North West including North Wales; North East; West Midlands; East Midlands; East Anglia; South; South West including South Wales; London. The regions were under the control of regional managers based at regional centres.

The £1,000 million mark had been achieved far more quickly than anyone had expected. But in five years, this total was to more than double. And this time it was foreseen. In an article in the Post and Times supplement, headed "How the Society broke the billion pound barrier", Norman Cowburn described the society's plan to put a new building on the Newton House site. It was to house computer staff and equipment so as to release accommodation in the main building for future growth. Cowburn closed his piece with these words:

"This development will be completed prior to celebrating the £2,000,000,000 milestone which we estimate will be in about five years time".

11: A Million Accounts

COWBURN'S PREDICTION was entirely right. The total was reached during 1983. By that time too, Britannia had passed another significant milestone — one million investment accounts. This success was achieved in an increasingly difficult environment. In 1980, Britannia was to experience one of those very rare moments in its history when withdrawals exceeded receipts.

The election of a Conservative Government in May 1979, committed to a policy of controlling the economy by monetarist policies, led to a steep rise in interest rates. In the government's first budget, minimum lending rate was raised from twelve to 14 per cent to curb the growth of lending in the banking sector. The Council of The Building Societies Association recommended a rise in the share rate from eight to 8.75 per cent from 1st August but hoped to stave off any decision on the mortgage rate until the new year. Britannia followed the share rate recommendation and kept its mortgage rate unchanged for existing borrowers. But the rate for new borrowers rose by 0.75 per cent to 12.5 per cent.

The figure of 12.5 per cent was the one the Council were planning for the following year. But the pressure of rising interest rates generally and competition from the ever growing range of rival savings schemes made even this figure look on the low side. The Conservatives had announced plans to give council tenants the right to buy their own homes, adding further pressure on a housing market where prices were rising rapidly because of inflation and increasing demand.

Sir Hubert issued a public warning that the coming mortgage rise could well be above 12.5 per cent. He stated his view that if many council tenants wanted to buy their own properties, building societies would have to seek extra funds from the City institutions.

"The result could be that mortgage rates would rise still further and probably lead to an extension of differential rates for larger mortgages".

Present money rates, he said, indicated that the cost of funds from the City would be above 15 per cent, implying a minimum mortgage rate of 16.5 per cent. He added: "Even if the cost were to be averaged with those for personal savings, the result would be a significant increase in the general mortgage rate".

The need to tap the City did not materialise but the higher mortgage rate did. In November, minimum lending rate shot up to 17 per cent. The Council responded by calling for a rise in the share rate to 10.5 per cent and in the mortgage rate to 15 per cent, a massive jump of 3.25 per cent. Even then it was feared that the rates were not high enough.

Britannia brought in the new share rate on 1st December increasing its range of other savings rates by a similar amount. The increase on existing mortgages was to apply from 1st January, 1980, and on new mortgages from 26th November of the current year.

By 1980, the situation was still deteriorating and for the first time since the society took the Britannia name, it found withdrawals exceeding receipts. The housebuilding background was similarly dismal. The total of houses built in 1979 was only 250,000 and only 136,000 of these were in the private sector. The pressures of demand and inflation had seen house prices rise by 30 per cent during the year.

In April, the society increased its rates on escalator bonds, and raised its limit on composite rate investments from £15,000 to £20,000. The limit for joint investors was raised from £30,000 to £40,000. The year saw two new developments which posed a threat to building society funds — the introduction of granny bonds and the move of the banks into the mortgage sector.

Britannia was among the leaders of the movement in counter-attacking the banks. In October, it produced a major innovation for the building society movement. A new two-month notice saving contract was launched, which paid 1.25 per cent above the usual rate for over the counter money. Offers of this kind were almost unknown before, with societies normally wanting money for a year if they were offering a higher than normal rate. And the extra rate offered usually amounted to just 0.5 per cent. Britannia's move was particularly provoked by the banks deciding to offer special terms for sums of around £2,000 lent to them for three or six months. National Savings certificates too were offering their highest-ever coupon rates. Besides posing a threat in the personal savings market, the banks also moved into the mortgage market, capturing 40 per cent of new mortgage lending at one stage in 1981. The pressure by the banks then wilted as they ran into their own problems in the difficult economic climate. First competition in borrowing slackened and then the banks found their new mortgage lending not quite so attractive in returns as they had hoped.

Despite the setback in 1980, Britannia's progress continued. The millionth investment account was opened in 1982, proof of the pulling power of Britannia's range of investment offers. Income once again exceeded withdrawals in 1981 — by a margin of £188 million.

The start of the interest rate crisis in 1979 coincided with Britannia's decision to end its membership of the local authority support scheme. The Council of The Building Societies Association had recommended that £400 million be made available by the scheme's members for the 1979/80 year. This would have effectively meant a doubling of Britannia's contribution. Britannia would have had to find another £1 million a month over and above its existing commitment of nearly £1 million. So Britannia decided to pull out entirely from 31st March, 1979. It felt it did enough already in the so-called "down market" lending sector. Its proportion of loans on pre-1919 houses had risen from under 19 per cent in 1974 to over 25 per cent in the third quarter of 1978.

At the society's annual meeting on 19th April, 1979, a change was agreed in the voting rules. Postal ballots for the office of director were ended, so that the decision was now taken at the annual meeting itself. The move was taken on the ground of increasing cost.

The social problems of present times were now affecting Britannia. Building society offices were becoming the target of raiders as well as the banks. Britannia pursued an active security policy of anti-bandit screens and alarms. In 1980, Newton House suffered its first hoax fire call which led to the building being evacuated and a thorough police search.

Newton House also saw an increasing number of visiting parties. School and college parties, and secretarial training groups were keen to see how a big building society worked in practice. But there were other more varied groups as well. On 1st October, 1979, a party of Vietnamese refugees were the guests of Britannia. The highlight of the following year was a visit on the 2nd May by a party of Americans under the auspices of the Rotary Club of Leek (Study Group Exchange Scheme).

The first royal visit to Newton House took place on the 24th November, 1981, when the Duke of Kent toured the building, accompanied by the Lord Lieutenant of Staffordshire, Sir Arthur Bryan. The Duke was introduced by Sir Hubert in the foyer to the society's executives and then escorted to the conference room on the first floor where Sir Hubert presented him to leading county, town and industrial personalities. Among the guests was Mr Thomas Ball, the general manager and secretary of the Leek United and Midlands. After lunch, Sir Hubert presented the Duke to members and former members of the staff.

Earlier in the year, Britannia took an interest in an unusual object for a building society — a model railway engine. The engine was a model of the Britannia steam locomotive built in 1951 and the first of a class of that name; it was hired for three years. The work of two brothers, Jim and Charles Hughes, it measured 14ft 6ins long, was one-fifth of actual size and weighed over a ton. It was exhibited in branch offices and at public events such as agricultural shows. The original locomotive was restored by the Britannia Locomotive Society and steamed up on 8th May, 1980. The loco was renamed Britannia two days later by her designer, Mr Robin Riddles, at a ceremony attended by Sir Hubert.

The Staffordshire base of Britannia was strengthened on 1st November, 1980, when the Stoke-on-Trent Permanent Building Society decided to join its giant neighbour. The Stoke society had been founded just before the Leek and Moorlands in 1852. Its assets at the handover totalled £3,500,000.

Britannia was called on next year to make another takeover of a society in difficulty as it had done on several occasions in the past. The society was the Alfreton Building Society whose assets were transferred on 30th April, 1981. Shortly afterwards, the former secretary of the society was to receive a three-year prison sentence for theft, forgery and falsification of accounts. The society had been founded in 1866 and its assets at the takeover were quite substantial — £5,400,000.

1982 saw another four societies come into Britannia. On the 31st March, the Wellington (Somerset and District) Building Society was absorbed. It dated from 1857 and its assets were £1,600,000. The following month the Denton Building Society (Manchester) came over. It had been established in 1865 and its assets at the transfer date of 30th April, were £340,000. On the 30th June, the Over Darwen Building Society of Darwen, with assets of £9,700,000 came over. It dated from 1869. On 31st October, the Driffield Building Society was absorbed. It dated from 1865 and its assets were £2,200,000.

1982 was quite an exceptional year for branch expansion. Besides the new branch offices created by the mergers, new offices were also opened in Alsager (Cheshire), Andover, Bedminster (Bristol), Cheadle (Cheshire), Chessington, Crosby (Liverpool), Hale (Cheshire), Ilkeston, Ipswich, Lanchester (Co Durham), Lincoln, Newton (Powys), Starbeck (Harrogate), Sudbury (Suffolk),

Wellingborough, West Ealing, Wombwell, and Worcester Park (London). The total number of branch offices now stood at 221. New agencies appointed during the year brought the total number of agents to over 600.

1983 saw the biggest merger since the Eastern Counties link-up. The Colne Building Society, with assets of £22,590,000, was absorbed on 1st April. It dated from 1866. On 1st May, the Welsh Economic Building Society of Pontypridd, dating from 1878, was absorbed. Its assets were £3,680,000. The Colne merger provided extra branch offices at Colne, Burnley, Burnley (Duke Bar), Bentham, Barnoldswick, Nelson (Brierfield), Clitheroe, Penwortham and Rawtenstall. The Welsh Economic merger gave Britannia a new branch office in Pontypridd, and other branch offices were opened in Ipswich (Queen Street), Portsmouth, Bridgend, Hythe, Wem (Salop), Hartshill and Wolstanton (Stoke-on-Trent), Hillsborough (Sheffield), Worksop and Warrington.

In Leek itself, a new branch office had been opened in 1980. The old Leek Baths in Derby Street had been demolished to make way for a new building to house the branch office. The former premises at 32 Derby Street, were bought by the government in June 1981 for conversion to a job centre.

In June 1980, Britannia moved in to buy a "protected" property adjoining Newton House. The property called Little Birchall Cottage was purchased for £20,000. It was sold again in October 1982, for £30,500, Britannia keeping part of the land. In 1980, Britannia also gave physical shape to its name by placing a bronze statue in the figure of Britannia in its courtyard. Some thought had been given to placing it at the front of the building but the directors believed it would be at risk from vandalism in such an open position. The enclosed courtyard was an ideal setting. The year also saw the major extension completed to Newton House to house the new computer complex.

In October 1982, Britannia decided to offload some of its Newton House administration tasks to the Ipswich head office. The mortgage administration and legal department of the NALGO business was transferred there, plus the legal deeds and mortgage accounts.

Sir Hubert Newton continued his role in the wider movement by becoming president of the Midland Association of Building Societies in 1979. On 31st May, 1979, Mr Travis Lyne, one of the deputy general managers, retired after 42 years' service. In November, Sir Desmond Heap retired from the board, having been a director since 1969. He had been knighted while a board member — in the New Year honours list of

1970. Donald Gould retired from the office of deputy chairman on 31st December and was succeeded by The Hon Peter Strutt, MC, a former director of the Eastern Counties society. At the following annual meeting in 1980, Gould along with Mr G. W. Pipe, also retired from the main board although he continued as chairman of the East Anglian Regional Board. On the 1st September, 1980, John Quipp, the deputy managing director, was appointed joint managing director, retiring from the post a year later on 9th September, 1981, when he reached the retirement age of 65. He continued as a director of the main board, as a consultant and as a member of the General Purposes Committee. The following month, Messrs G. Belfield, R. S. Green, and J. R. Griffiths, were promoted from assistant to deputy general managers. John Quipp was to become deputy chairman in 1983 when The Hon Peter Strutt stepped down from the post.

In March 1982, Britannia said farewell to George Lees, deputy general manager, who had brought the NALGO society into the Leek fold in July, 1960. The next month, the board suffered the loss of Lord Greenwood, who died on 12th April. The board decided after Greenwood's death to reduce the number of directors laid down in its rules from eleven to ten.

On the 22nd April, Sir Hubert was prevented by ill-health from attending the annual meeting. It was the first time he had been absent since he came to Leek in 1933. In the autumn, a much-prized honour fell his way. He became president of Stoke City Football Club which he had followed keenly since 1933. Another local honour bestowed on him was the Mayoralty of The Ancient Corporation of Hanley in 1981, an historic but nominal post.

Two important changes in standard building society practice came in the early 1980s. In 1981, the board agreed that every applicant for a mortgage should receive a copy of the valuer's report following widespread press and political debate on the subject. In 1982, borrowers were allowed to insure their properties with insurance companies of their own choosing. In the same year, Britannia joined the Building Societies Investors Protection Scheme, set up because of the Grays and Wakefield collapses.

The 15 per cent mortgage rate lasted until 1st March, 1981, when it was cut by one per cent. Britannia applied this date for existing borrowers although it allowed the new rate on mortgages from the end of December 1980. The share rate dropped to 9.25 per cent from 1st February, 1980. Rates fell again on 1st April, the share rate dropping to 8.5 per cent and the mortgage rate for existing borrowers to 13 per cent, although new borrowers enjoyed the reduction from 17th March. The trend of reducing interest rates was reversed later in the year, and the mortgage rate jumped by two per cent on 1st December, back to the 15 per cent level. The share rate had gone up to 9.75 per cent from 1st November.

1982 saw rates falling again with three changes in the year. The share rate fell to 8.75 per cent, then 7.75 per cent and lastly to 6.25 per cent on 1st December. The mortgage rate also came down to ten per cent by 1st December, having dropped in stages to 13.5 per cent and twelve per cent. Whether the times were good or bad, building societies now realised that stable rates were a thing of the distant past.

From 1st February, 1982, the board stopped its differential charging scheme on mortgages, applying special rates only on sums above £50,000.

It was not only the changes of rate that made building society business complex. Each time the rate changed, not only the share rate and mortgage rate but a host of other rates had to change too. Competition in the personal savings market was now so intense that the building societies had to fight off their rivals with a package of investment offers. When Britannia changed its general share rate to 6.25 per cent on 1st December, 1982, it had to change rates on ten other categories of investment. The full table was (rates in brackets refer to closed investment issues.):

Shares	6.25 per cent
Shares at 3 months' notice	(7.25 per cent)
Shares at 2 months' notice — opened prior to 1st December	(7.5 per cent)
Shares at two months' notice — opened from 1st December	7.25 per cent
Regular savings — opened prior to 1st December	(7.5 per cent)
Regular savings — opened from 1st December	7.25 per cent
Escalator bonds	(6.75 per cent to 9.25 per cent)
5 year Option bonds	(8.25 per cent)
1 year Option bonds — 1st September issue	(7.75 per cent)
1 year Option bonds — 1st December issue	7.25 per cent
Personal deposits	6 per cent

An important investment concession was granted by the Inland Revenue in September when the maximum permitted holding for individual investors was increased to £30,000 and for joint investors to £60,000.

The years 1982 and 1983 recorded exactly the same growth in assets — 19.1 per cent. The 1983 rise took the Britannia past the £2,000 million mark. The asset figure at the end of 1983 was £2,376,351,000 against £1,995,167,000 at the 1982 year-end. A few further statistics on the 1983 year show the size of the Britannia operation. Incoming investment from the million – plus depositors totalled £1,317,519,000, including £96,471,000 interest credited. Withdrawals by investors totalled £980,075,000. The sum advanced on mortgages was £459,511,000 and the number of mortgages completed came to 24,850.

On 5th April, yet another new investment package was offered. A three year term bond was introduced at a guaranteed differential interest rate of 1.25 per cent over the ordinary rate. A new one year option bond was also introduced with the same differential. A new differential mortgage rates scheme was brought in on the same date. The ten per cent interest figure on an advance up to £25,000 went up to 10.5 per cent between £25,001 and £50,000. The figure between £50,001 and £60,000 was eleven per cent. Above that was by arrangement. The limit on mortgage interest relief was increased in the budget by £5,000 to £30,000.

Mr Samuel Green and Mr Wallace Morfey retired from the board at the annual meeting. Mr Philip Taylor, a director of 34 years' standing, retired in September.

In their place came Mr David Berriman, aged 55, and Mr Stephen Sebire, aged 46. Berriman was a director of the merchant bankers, Guinness Mahon, and of the major communications company, Cable and Wireless. Sebire was managing director of Berisfords Ltd, of Congleton. The new appointments were part of a conscious decision by the board to lower the average age of the directors by recruiting younger men, particularly those with experience in business, finance and modern technology.

In 1984, the policy was pursued further with the appointments of The Earl of Shrewsbury, aged 32, and of Mr John Hill, aged 49. The Earl of Shrewsbury was a vice-president of the Midland Association of Building Societies and well-known in farming and landowning circles, particularly in Staffordshire and Shropshire. Hill was a consultant with PA Management Services. A native of Leek, he now lived in Guildford in Surrey. The changes at the 1984 annual meeting coincided with the retirements of Mr Henry Warner and Mr Ronald Willett.

Britannia was called on in 1983 to face wider changes in the building society movement. Mortgage Interest Relief At Source (MIRAS) was introduced by the government, whereby tax relief was deducted from the mortgage payment instead of from the borrower's personal tax assessment. The change placed a heavy burden on Britannia's organisation as it did on those of its rival societies.

In October 1983, the interest rate cartel system, so long opposed by Sir Hubert, was replaced by so-called "advised rates". The previous requirement to give 28 days notice of any change was scrapped although societies were encouraged to give notice of their intentions.

A debate about the future of the movement was started in January when The Building Societies Association published a paper on "The Future Constitution and Powers of Building Societies". The document was a response to pressure by the Conservative Government which sought reform of the country's financial services. The government's object was to make them more competitive and to equalise tax and other concessions. Severe competition from the banking sector had been one of the main features of building society life in the early 1980s along with the growth of computerisation. Now the societies were to ask themselves how far they had travelled down the road to becoming virtual banks themselves with their instant withdrawal facilities and their many savings packages.

Britannia cut its last remaining links with its old headquarters at New Stockwell House in 1984, when the remaining two houses in the society's ownership at the rear of the building were sold to the district council. Newton House remained a centre of attraction for visitors. In April, 1984, a party of Canadian Rotarians visiting Leek were welcomed to the building.

In March 1984, Sir Hubert became a member of the Building Societies Members Association — a body formed to protect the interests of members of building societies.

Britannia also took the decision to install cash dispensing machines at certain branches by joining the "Link" consortium of societies and banks for the installation of automatic teller machines.

A new investment package reducing investment account rates was brought in from 1st May, coinciding with a cut of one per cent in the mortgage rate. In August, investment rates went up again — by 1.5 per cent. Mortgages rose by 2.5 per cent. On 17th September, there were further increases in Britannia's seven-day and 28-day notice accounts.

In December, rates fell again with a one per cent cut all round in both investment rates and mortgages.

In July, another important innovation took place with a pilot scheme in the Southern region for the issue of American Express travellers cheques.

The end of the year saw the retirement of Norman Cowburn as managing director, although he remained a board member.

During 1984, new branch offices had been opened at Girvan in Ayrshire, Govan Cross (Glasgow) and Hucknall in Nottinghamshire.

The highlight of the year for Britannia was a documentary programme by Granada Television on the society. It was shown on all commercial channels on Sunday, 22nd July. It outlined the many facets of the society's work and its leading role in a movement that was changing rapidly.

12: Into the Future

BRITANNIA TODAY is not just a very different creature from the old Leek and Moorlands society and its other ancestors such as the Eastern Counties and the Westbourne Park. It is a very different creature from the society of just a decade ago. The pressure of the financial markets and the growth in computerisation have changed methods of working in dramatic fashion. Britannia is now a modern financial enterprise and the degree of business and administrative expertise needed is growing all the time. The growth of a range of savings packages, the computerisation of the society's finances and the growth of ancillary activities such as printing have all placed increased demands upon the organisation.

Today, there is a wide range of different savings schemes to meet the needs of many different kinds of investors. These savings schemes can be grouped under five main headings — General Investment Share Account, Deposit Account, Regular Savings, Save As You Earn, and High Interest Accounts.

The General Investment Share Account has been the main source of funds over the years. Anybody can become a member of the society by investing at least £1 in a share account. Withdrawals can normally be made on demand, except in the case of very large sums. The interest is calculated on the balance in the account at the close of business each day and is usually added to the balance of the account twice a year.

The Deposit Account is operated in the same way as a share account but attracts a lower rate of interest. Limited companies, clubs, associations etc investing in the society must use deposit accounts. They cannot become members through the share scheme.

Regular Savings accounts are for members who want to save a regular amount each month but require only limited withdrawal facilities. A higher rate of interest is paid than on ordinary share accounts and the account can be closed at any time without penalty.

The Save As You Earn scheme is controlled by Statute and is designed for people who wish to save a regular amount for five years. After the five-year period has expired, the balance earns additional bonuses for each year the account remains open for up to a further four years.

High interest accounts are for members wishing to invest large sums or who are prepared to give long notice of withdrawals. Britannia also offers payment of interest each month, instead of half-yearly, on many accounts.

The lending of funds takes two main forms — the normal mortgage and the endowment mortgage. The normal mortgage loan is usually repaid over a period of up to 25 years. Nowadays, most borrowers make the repayment each month through an automatic bank or giro transfer. The previous system was for borrowers to present their mortgage subscription card to be updated when making payments each month. This system still operates but is dying out.

An endowment mortgage is for borrowers who take out an endowment assurance policy with an insurance company. It guarantees that on the maturity of the policy, the capital realised is used to pay off the mortgage debt to the society. The balance outstanding on the loan does not therefore reduce, and a slightly higher rate of interest is charged than on an ordinary mortgage. Because the policy is a life assurance one, the mortgage debt is also repaid if the borrower dies before the policy matures.

Members' and borrowers' business can normally be carried out at either the branches or agencies or at Newton House or Ipswich, but very large withdrawals are only processed at Leek and Ipswich. Mortgage applications and redemptions are processed partly by branches and partly at Leek and Ipswich. The closure of SAYE accounts is confined only to the two head offices. Otherwise every branch offers a full range of services and members' passbooks are completely interchangeable between branches and agencies.

Britannia has led the way in the building society movement in computerising transactions between the customer at the branch office window and the head office. But the challenge to management has not just been in computer techniques. It has had to rethink all aspects of personnel policy to meet the new competitive environment. And the sheer scale of transactions has meant management having to develop expertise in the ancillary areas such as printing. The volume of printing required is now enormous, and with the constant changes in interest rates, the printing task has become much more complex. Frequent updates have to be sent to customers based on computer assessment of their new mortgage terms when interest rates change.

The growth of the printing operation was inextricably linked to the computerisation programme started in 1970, which soon began to generate a large amount of standard computerised information for the business and for customers. During the 1960s, the Leek society had maintained its account records on ledger accounting machines, and transactions were handled semi-automatically. There were 15 accounting centres and a variety of machines were in use. Some used a magnetic stripe on the ledger card to read the date and balance.

The society made its first move into the world of computerisation in 1969 when it recruited its first computer staff. The following year, it purchased an ICL System 4/40 machine, followed by a System 4/72 model in 1973. The task of the first computer was to transfer onto a central computer record all the society's accounting previously handled at twelve centres throughout the country. This was tackled in the second half of the year according to very tight schedules. It was essential that the schedules were kept to because of decimalisation of the currency the following year. The deadlines were met and decimalisation passed off with no problems.

The 4/40 system worked on magnetic tape files. Staff obtained account details by submitting a written request which was then processed in a batch with other requests. The account details were printed centrally and distributed. This was a major administrative advance but absurdly slow compared to the computer technology of the mid-1980s. The delay from request to delivery of the account was in the order of several hours.

After the basic accounting functions were computerised by the 4/40 system, a number of systems to cope with the society's special requirements at quarter-end, half-year-end, and year-end were developed. Statistical systems to provide information for management were also worked out.

The slowness of the 4/40 system meant inevitably it would be replaced after a few years as computer technology accelerated. The more powerful 4/72 system installed in 1973 was much closer to the computer technology we know today. It provided rapid inquiry facilities using visual display units.

After its installation, the majority of the departments at Newton House were provided with their own specially tailored systems. This enabled them to access and examine account records, change those records in response to members' requests and transactions, and to produce standard computerised letters. Some of the departmental systems even provided a diary service to action a specified activity on a particular day. The results produced by computerisation were dramatic. By 1976, the staff at Newton House and Ipswich to which the system was extended, remained almost unchanged in numbers yet there had been a 70 per cent increase in the workload.

This office record information system run by the 4/72 computer, based on visual display units in the departments, was called ARTEMIS (Advanced Real-Time Express Mortgage and Investment System). A real-time system is defined as one in which the user has a terminal linked direct to the computer through which he or she can interrogate and amend records. The cost at the time was £750,000.

At the start of computerisation, the society had been behind many of its rivals but in the mid-1970s, it overtook them in one big leap. By 1975, many of the other major building societies had started to install computer terminals in their branches, connected by Post Office lines to their main computer centres. These terminals not only enabled information to be fed to the building society's head office but also provided a means of answering enquiries made at the branch by members as to the state of their accounts. Britannia decided to go a stage further and use the next step in the logical development of the system — the direct processing of transactions by computer at the counter. Under this system, even the total in the individual member's account and the interest due would be printed by computer at the counter in his or her passbook.

The society carried out an extensive investigation into the best system available to do this task. It turned out that there was no British equipment available. So equipment supplied by the Swedish computer concern, Datasaab, was used. The new system was called MIDAS (Mortgage and Investment Direct Administration System). It was first installed in the Leek branch office in September 1977, and was so successful that it was rapidly extended throughout the branch system. The move put Britannia in the forefront of the computer revolution, leading the way for the other societies to follow.

In 1980, Britannia bought its present computer, an ICL 2972, capable of one million instructions a second. This could handle all anticipated growth in the computer system through the 1980s.

Britannia's system has the records of investment accounts on central computer files. Every night from Monday to Friday, the central files are updated, feeding in the details of new accounts, transactions (receipts and withdrawals) and so-called "static" data amendments such as changes in names and addresses. The system centres on the daily maintenance of the main account files — investment and mortgage. In addition to these main files, several subsidiary files are also run daily.

Among the other systems run is a range of weekly, monthly, quarterly, half-yearly and yearly systems, some of which update the main files while others only extract data and report on the status of the files. There is a special suite of computer programmes designed to cope with Britannia's extensive merger activity. When the society absorbs another, the suite is run through the computer to take the new account details on to Britannia's main files. If the mortgage rate changes, another system notifies all borrowers of the revised payments and adjusts their mortgage account accordingly.

Every minute of the working day, an average of 240 data messages "hit" the computer system. Money transactions form most of the messages and most of these are from branches on the MIDAS system. Only one branch at the time of writing still remains without MIDAS and it is soon to be converted.

Bank transactions (standing order, third-party credits, etc.) or Giro transactions are received encoded on a reel of magnetic tape. They are input directly into the system as are magnetic tapes containing transactions from organisations taking part in those Britannia savings schemes where deductions are made direct from salary and credited to a Britannia account. The transactions are recorded by the computer on a reel of magnetic tape and held there until close of business at 5 p.m. each evening when the reel is used to update the main file.

At each branch office on the MIDAS system, a mini-computer controls the operation of the equipment connecting the branch with Newton House. Each cashier has a transaction keyboard with keypad and indicator with lights. The cashier shares an alphabetic keyboard and the passbook printer with another cashier. The printer has a so-called "journal roll" on which all transactions, new account and static amendment details are recorded and a tally roll on which system messages are printed. The printer can print a variety of documents, including passbook entries, cheques, withdrawal forms, receipts, sticky labels and cashiers' total returns. Each branch has its own magnetic storage (cassette tape or diskette) which is used to record data if the link between the head office computer and the branch is severed for any reason.

MIDAS provides all the procedures necessary for dealing with customers' accounts. Cashier totals are maintained for each cashier, and branch totals are produced at the end of the day after all cashiers have balanced. Full security is provided and a cashier must have a key and the knowledge of a secret security number before getting access to

Section of the Typing Pool, Newton House.

Michael Shaw, FCA,
Chief General Manager, 1982-185,
Managing Director, 1985-.

Sir Hubert Newton, September 1983.

MIDAS. Certain functions and withdrawals over an audit limit require a supervisor key.

The basic reason for computerisation is cost saving and much quicker customer service. But it also provides greater security for customers and greater accuracy with much less risk of mistakes. It is of immense value too in monitoring the society's cash flow and its investment holdings.

The ICL 2972 will make possible further technical advance. It enables files to be updated in "real time". That means that transactions and static amendments can be put on the main files as and when they occur instead of each night in a batch update. The 2972 can also store far greater quantities of information than its predecessors. This means better inquiry and search facilities. As file organisation techniques improve under the 2972, management will be able to control and monitor branch activity and cash flow more accurately.

The communications network between Newton House and the branches will become more sophisticated still. It will soon become possible for members to examine their account details and make transactions from their homes, places of work, shops and any other places served by a telephone and a computer data entry terminal. This will cut down the need for members to actually visit branches and cut down on correspondence with the head offices.

The society started its own printing operation in March 1972, using an area previously used by the accounts department at the former head office in New Stockwell House. At that time, the machinery comprised just one offset litho printing press, a small guillotine and a couple of items of ancillary equipment. Now the printing department has expanded to take in most of the printing needs of the huge Britannia operation. After the merger with the Eastern Counties Building Society, a major in-house printing development programme was started. In 1975, the directors approved the purchase of a two-colour press, a larger guillotine and several items of finishing equipment. The new machinery was fully compatible with the existing equipment.

The department moved to Sneyd Street in 1976 when New Stockwell House was bought by the Staffordshire Moorlands District Council. Typesetting, camera and darkroom facilities were added to the operation, together with a larger litho press and a letterpress platen. The extension to Newton House brought the department in with the main head office operation. A major appraisal of the society's printing needs was carried out during 1982 and 1983. The volume of work had completely saturated the capacity of the plant. The growing intricacy of the work, particularly the colour printing, demanded more sophisticated machinery.

A full costing exercise followed on the appraisal, and the result was that the existing printing machines were replaced with Heidelberg machines. At the same time, the typesetting machines were replaced, and a new guillotine installed. A seven-station collating machine was bought with a folding and stitching unit. So Britannia is now equipped with the latest in printing machine technology, and it is vitally needed. With a million investment accounts, changing of the share rate itself involves a gigantic printing and addressing operation, apart from the normal day-to-day business requirements and the general production of publicity material.

In its personnel policy, Britannia has developed along four fronts — the working environment, promotional opportunities, welfare and the training function itself. Training is recognised not as an end in itself but as the means by which staff can develop their particular talents. After the opening of Newton House in 1970, a programme of training at all staff levels was put into effect and courses held regularly for branch managers and other staff. The courses include tutorial and discussion groups, and provide the valuable opportunity for branch office and headquarters staff to get to know each other, so unifying the society and giving it an identity of purpose across the country. It is essential that staff, whether in Belfast or Inverness or Torquay or Carmarthen or other towns far distant from Newton House, share and feel this identity. A training department was started in 1978 to design specialised courses both at Newton House and over the rest of the country. The latest aids are now used in training — videos, overhead projectors and other audio-visual equipment.

Staff are also encouraged to pursue studies for the many professional courses now available, and some are granted day release. A close working relationship has been formed with the Leek College of Further Education in business and secretarial studies courses. The society follows a policy of trying to promote staff from within its own organisation and great value is placed on this career structure.

The emphasis inside Britannia is on a total "employment" package. Staff receive mortgage help, cheap canteen facilities, BUPA membership, and membership of the sports and social club. The staff magazine, *Roundabout,* provides news of staff activity throughout the country.

But it is not just in the growth and complexity of its organisation that Britannia is facing a challenging and testing time. Soon it will have to make a decision about what sort of animal it wants to be in the years to the turn of the century as the building society movement contemplates the biggest changes yet in its entire history.

The ease of withdrawals has long meant that the societies have given a service in many ways similar to a banking service. The difference has been that societies have not been able to offer, under building society law, direct banking and cheque book facilities on their own. For example, a society cannot issue a cheque guarantee card because it would be promising to meet a payment to a third party whether or not sufficient funds were in the individual account. It has no legal power to do this. Nor can societies enter into reciprocal arrangements with each other for providing an encashment and banking service for each other's customers.

The latest computer developments are starting to blur these distinctions between bank accounts and building society accounts. Not only are some building societies allying with banks to offer cheque book facilities but some are pioneering the way in the latest money transmission services. Cash dispensing machines are now being operated by several societies, and some societies are leaping into the future of automated cashless banking by trial schemes where computer credit machines in shops deduct money from accounts without cash changing hands. A magnetic disk or card is simply inserted into the machine, carrying the customer's account total on a magnetic code. The account is then debited automatically by the amount of the transaction.

Britannia was the pioneer of the "front desk to computer" instant accounting systems for building societies. The "cashless" shopping transaction is no more essentially than a development of this. Britannia has yet to decide how far it wants to go down this road into automated banking. But the choice before it is far more wideranging than this.

At the time of writing (1985), fundamental changes in the laws governing building societies are being considered by the government and The Building Societies Association. These changes will allow societies to become financial conglomerates offering a far greater range of services to investors. So societies will have more than just automated banking to consider. They will have to decide how much they want to remain pure building societies working to the former rules and how much they want to take advantage of the new opportunities the government wants to open up.

The government is examining areas relating to housing finance which, it believes, the building societies should expand into — such as estate agency, conveyancing, property management and residential property development. It is examining how to give the societies direct and wideranging powers to take on banking functions, including the right to issue cheque books in the same way as the banks, backed up by the societies' own cheque guarantee cards. The Building Societies Association has further suggested that societies should be allowed to go into direct insurance broking because the societies act as intermediaries in respect of insurance related to their main business, such as mortgage protection policies, house insurance and endowment mortgages.

The first signs of this pending revolution in building society practice came in a Building Societies Association discussion document in January 1983. A further document was published in February 1984, entitled "New Legislation for Building Societies", which took into account comments made on the 1983 document. A government Green Paper followed in July 1984. It discussed the content of the two documents and raised further issues such as the supervision of the wider financial powers envisaged for the movement.

The existing statement of building society objectives is in section 1 of the 1962 Building Societies Act. It reads:

"The purpose for which a society may be established under this Act is that of raising, by the subscriptions of the members, a stock or fund for making advances to members out of the funds of the society upon security by way of mortgage of freehold or leasehold estate".

A society's powers of action are limited to this purpose. What the government is seeking is an amendment of section 1 so that a society's primary purpose, but not sole purpose, is the raising of funds from individual members for lending on security by mortgage of owner-occupied residential property. A society would then have the powers to engage in other activities which would be set out in a list, the contents of which could be varied from time to time dependent upon Parliamentary approval. Under the government's plans, up to ten per cent of a society's commercial assets could be in these other areas. Commercial assets are defined as assets other than liquid assets and fixed assets such as office premises.

The crucial part of the new proposals for Britannia is that there would be an elite group of the leading building societies who would be given much wider powers than the rest. This group is defined as societies with free reserves of more than £3 million.

The powers which are likely to be given will not be compulsorily enforced. It will be up to the societies to choose which if any of the new powers they want to take on. But for leading societies such as Britannia, there will be no stepping back in the new freer environment from taking on at least some of the new powers, if only in self protection against the rivalry of others.

Already the government has made a start at the time of writing on one of its major objectives — the equalisation of tax treatment between the building societies and other financial sectors. Building societies from April 1985, have had to pay corporation tax on profits from the holding of government stocks, and the clearing banks in turn now pay the composite rate tax on deposit interest.

The building societies can undoubtedly easily handle most of the extra services the government wants them to handle. What causes most concern is the new element of asset risk outside their present experience.

The powers envisaged in the Green Paper for direct ownership of land and of residential property will certainly require greater reserve ratios. Building society executives will have to learn a new expertise in this area. The present bar to building societies holding land followed the collapse of the Liberator Building Society and its imprudent property deals towards the end of the last century. The State Building Society collapse in 1959 was because of lending to property companies and showed the modern-day risks involved. The powers of direct land ownership would only be open to the leading societies (such as Britannia), with £3 million or more in free reserves. They would be accompanied by much stricter powers of supervision by the Chief Registrar.

The power of unsecured lending would be a similar prerogative for this group of elite societies. This consumer lending would be aimed at housing-related items, such as furniture, fittings and repairs. This is something that the building societies are probably already providing in effect in some cases, but within the amount of the loan secured on the first mortgage. In the view of the government, unsecured loan finance on a shorter term may be a more sensible way of paying for some small home improvement and repairs, than a full mortgage.

The problem is that building society liquidity margins and reserve ratios stand well below those of the banks because of the stability of their business. Once the societies take on such banking functions, then higher ratios will be needed. The accompanying proposals to allow building societies to offer direct credit card and cheque guarantee services is part of the same problem. To offer these services directly, overdraft facilities, even if minimal, have to be offered to the customer. A credit card or cheque guarantee card would be valueless if there was not an unsecured borrowing facility to support it. The government's proposals suggest an additional overdraft guarantee scheme so that the smaller societies not in the elite group, can also provide such facilities.

For the general unsecured lending powers of the elite societies, the government envisages a limit of £5,000 on advances to any one individual, while the societies build up their expertise in this area. Overall limits as a percentage of assets are proposed to cover three categories — unsecured lending, ownership of property and land, and equity investment, for example if building societies use their new powers to set up insurance company subsidiaries.

How will Britannia fare in this brave new world that is opening up before it? It has strengths both in its traditions and its role as a leading innovator in the movement. Change is something it has never feared, but the innovations it has made have always been according to the tried and trusted methods of building society finance. Under the government's proposals, those methods will be changed irretrievably. New areas of decision on lending principles will be opened up.

When the changes come, Sir Hubert Newton will have severed his last official connections with the society. Norman Cowburn retired at the end of 1984. It will be left to new men to carry on Britannia's tradition of sound finance and competitive innovation. Decisions as crucial as any in the past will have to be taken about Britannia's future.

It is, of course, impossible to predict how Britannia will develop its new powers. Newton and Cowburn have long campaigned for greater freedom for societies and many of the changes would have been welcome to them. But both men are unhappy about the proposals for building societies to go into the consumer credit market. Already there are signs that this may over-inflate consumer credit rather than add welcome diversity. It is not uncommon these days for 100 per cent mortgages to be granted, for insurance companies to write excess risks, and for people to be persuaded into taking out life cover when their commitments are high enough already. Some societies are, even now, co-operating with hire purchase companies in order to get a part of the hire purchase business in furniture, carpets and other goods new houseowners need — adding by the very generous credit terms offered to the risk of over-commitment by borrowers.

It is this issue of over-commitment which worries Newton and Cowburn most. Freer lending not only carries financial risks for the building society movement. It also requires higher standards still of responsibility to the borrower. Britannia and its predecessor societies have always upheld the highest standards of responsibility. Those standards have made it one of the strongest and most stable building societies in the movement. Its strength is the result of its 128-year history going back to those first meetings of a few forward thinking people in a small Staffordshire town. The values of Britannia and its predecessors have been the solid, reliable dependable values of small town England.

The parting of Newton and Cowburn, chairman and chief executive respectively, in the same year, marks a watershed in Britannia's history. The parting of Newton closes a 51-year chapter of the society's history which has seen it become a truly nationwide society. Sir Hubert has always had a sense of occasion as his tenure of the highest offices in the movement and his organisation of its major events — national and international — have amply demonstrated. With the fundamental changes about to come in building society practice, his parting is the symbol of a change in eras not only for Britannia itself but for the whole movement. Alongside other such greats of the movement as Enoch Hill of the Halifax and Harold Bellman of the Abbey National, he will go down in its annals as one of its foremost leaders and innovators.

The history of Britannia has seen almost uninterrupted success and rarely failure. That success is because the society has always been forward looking. How else could a society based in such a small town have grown as it did? The qualities needed to sustain that success are needed now as ever they have been in the past. Britannia is ready to take another step in its distinguished history.

Appendix 1

DIRECTORS, EXECUTIVES, PATRONS and TRUSTEES 1856-1985

Patrons

1859-1867	Lord Ingestre, MP
1859-1895	Smith Child (Baronet 1867-1894; MP 1867-1871)
1859-1866	John Cruso
1859-1863	Charles Flint
1859-1861	John Davenport
1859-1870	M. Gaunt
1859-1871	Rev. John Sneyd
1861-1872	A. J. Worthington
1861-1866	William Evans
1864-1881	Sir Edward Buller (MP 1864-1871)
1867-1876	Rt.-Hon. The Earl of Shrewsbury
1867-1869	Robert Broome
1867-1901	John Robinson

Trustees

1856	Thomas Birch
1856-1884	Joshua Brough
1856-1877	George Hammersley
1856-1862	Robert Hammersley
1856-1866	Charles Heaton
1856-1863	James Mycock
1860-1889	John Ward, JP
1867-1876	Dr. Heaton
1869-1873	Richard Turnock
1880-1929	Sir Arthur Nicholson, JP, CC
1890-1926	Anthony Ward, JP, CC

Presidents

1856-1879	George Hammersley
1918-1929	Sir Arthur Nicholson, JP, CC
1929-1932	Henry Salt
1932-1934	Alfred Moore, JP
1934-1938	William Hassall, JP
1938-1961	Sir Ernest Johnson, JP
1961-1962	Gilbert Tatton
1962-1964	Sir Bernard White, KBE
1985-	Sir Hubert Newton, Hon MA (Keele), FCIS, FCBSI

Honorary Life President

1974-1985	Sir Clavering Fison, DL (Chairman of the Eastern Counties Building Society Board from 1944-1966; Honorary Life President, 1966-1974)

Vice-Presidents

1918-1924	Admiral Sir Guy Gaunt, KCMG, CB
1918-1931	Robert Heath, JP, DL, CC
1918-1949	G. Fletcher Bagshaw, MBE, FAI
1918-1935	John Knight
1925-1928	Arthur S. Boucher, JP
1925-1928	Charles Birch, JP, CC
1925-1926	William Edward Challinor, JP
1926-1955	John Ward, JP
1928-1967	Lt.-Col. W. J. Challinor, DSO, MA, JP
1930-1931	G. Ernest Watson, JP
1934-1939	John H. Wain
1934-1943	Col. The Rt.-Hon. Josiah C. Wedgwood, DSO, MP
1934-1963	S. Myott, JP
1936-1952	Frank G. Johnson, BA
1940-1949	Albert Cook, JP
1944-1949	Ernest C. Astle

Chairmen

1856-1879	George Hammersley
1879-1890	John Ward, JP
1890-1912	Sir Arthur Nicholson, JP, CC
1912-1926	Henry Salt
1927-1934	Alfred Moore, JP
1934-1938	William Hassall, JP
1938-1945	Lt.-Col. Guy Worthington, MA
1945-1962	Gilbert Tatton
1962-1964	Sir Bernard White, KBE
1964-1965	Hubert Newton, FCIS, FCBSI
1965-1966	Lord Hurd
1966-1974	Sir Hubert Newton, Hon. MA (Keele), FCIS, FCBSI (Knighted June 1968)
1974-1976	Rt.-Hon. Lord Greenwood of Rossendale, PC, MA, JP, DL
1976-1985	Sir Hubert Newton, Hon. MA (Keele), FCIS, FCBSI
1985-	John Quipp, ACBSI

Deputy Chairmen (1956 on)

1956-1962	Sir Bernard White, KBE
1962-1966	Hubert Newton, FCIS, FBS
1966-1967	Edward Moody, FCCS, FCBSI
1967-1974	Brigadier Edwin Flavell, DSO, MC, TD, DL
1974-1975	Sir Hubert Newton, Hon. MA (Keele), FCIS, FCBSI
1974-1979	Donald Gould, FCBSI
1980-1982	The Hon. Peter Strutt, MC
1983-1985	John Quipp, ACBSI
1985-	E. W. Wallaker, FSVA

Directors

1856-1859	Joseph Bentley
1856-1861	James Bermingham
1856-1864	Robert Fergyson
1856-1879	George Hammersley
1856	Thomas Johnson
1856	Peter Magnier, Jnr.
1856-1860	John Mathews
1856-1871	William Sherratt Mollatt
1856-1863	James Mycock
1856-1868	George Nall
1856-1894	William Barlow Nixon
1856-1913	Thomas Shaw
1856-1864	W. M. Sugden
1856-1863	John Walmsley
1856-1861	J. T. Warrington
1856-1857	Thomas West
1857-1859	William Putman
1858-1861	George Tipper
1858-1860	Joseph Burton
1860-1900	John Brealey, JP
1860-1893	Stephen Goodwin
1860-1874	J. S. Winfield
1861-1867	Richard Turnock
1862-1864	Isaac Cope
1862-1864	John James Ritche
1862-1900	Samuel Travis
1864	George Burton
1865-1905	Robert Farrow
1865-1874	W. M. Hilliard
1865-1876	Joshua Nicholson
1866-1868	R. M. Fergyson
1866-1890	John Hill
1868-1869	Ralph Mountfort, Jnr.
1868-1873	James Trythall
1869-1877	Thomas S. Hallowes
1872-1873	Thomas Brealey
1874-1897	Henry Bermingham
1874-1921	Edwin Phillips
1875-1880	James Hayward
1876-1918	Robert Wright, JP
1879-1890	J. F. Nixon
1879-1932	Henry Salt
1881-1908	William H. Hartley
1891-1893	W. H. Broster
1891-1929	Arthur H. Shaw
1894-1899	Arthur W. Goodwin
1894-1899	R. M. Fergyson
1898-1907	Henry Eddowes

1901-1902	Joseph Hill
1901-1928	James Morton
1902-1927	George Hammersley
1902-1934	Alfred Moore, JP
1903-1917	Thomas Robinson
1906-1931	Reginald W. Brealey
1907-1938	William Hassall, JP, CC
1908-1922	Edward Keates
1913-1928	Lt.-Col. W. F. Challinor, DSO
1918-1939	Fred Carding, JP
1919-1928	H. E. Whittles
1921-1935	F. L. Burton
1922-1950	S. M. Phillips
1928-1970	Lt.-Col. Guy Worthington, MA
1928-1949	D. Fergyson
1928-1946	H. J. Arundel
1928-1940	C. Birch, JP, CC
1929-1940	Col. A. F. Nicholson, TD, JP, DL
1931-1955	G. Ernest Watson, JP
1931-1946	G. H. Sheldon, JP
1935-1942	W. A. Furmston
1936-1956	F. Leslie Davenport, JP
1938-1985	Sir Hubert Newton, Hon. MA (Keele), FCIS, FCBSI
1939-1970	Harvey Leek
1939-1953	James Pilkington
1940-1962	Gilbert Tatton
1940-1944	Edgar Henshaw
1946-1963	William D. Walker, JP
1949-1957	G. Fletcher Bagshaw, MBE, FAI
1950-1983	P. H. Taylor, TD, FRICS, FAI (Hons.)
1955-1964	Sir Bernard White, KBE
1959-1972	M. A. Tatton
1959-1966	R. C. D. Todd
1963-1977	Sidney Hill
1964-1983	S. S. Green, BSc
1969-1979	Sir Desmond Heap, LLM, Hon. LLD
1972-1982	Rt.-Hon. Lord Greenwood of Rossendale, PC, MA, JP, DL
1972-	E. W. Wallaker, FSVA
1977-	Norman Cowburn, FCIS, FCBSI
1977-	John Quipp, ACBSI
1983-	D. Berriman, MA, FIB, CBIM
1983-	S. J. Sebire
1984-	John Hill, MA, CEng, MI, MECH E, MIMC
1984-	The Earl of Shrewsbury and Waterford
1965-1977	Brigadier Edwin Flavell, DSO, MC, TD, DL (Director, Westbourne Park Building Society 1961-1965)
1965-1977	M. A. Nelson (Director, Westbourne Park Building Society 1964-1965)
1965-1968	Edward Moody (Director, Westbourne Park Building Society 1965)

1974-1983	Ald. W. M. Morfey, MBE, MA, JP (Director, Eastern Counties Building Society 1967-1974, Ipswich Permanent Benefit Building Society 1951-1967)
1974-	The Hon. Peter Strutt, MC (Director, Eastern Counties Building Society 1959-1974)
1974-1984	R. H. Willett, FRICS (Director, Eastern Counties Building Society 1967-1974, Ipswich Permanent Benefit Building Society 1959-1967)
1974-1984	H. A. Warner, DSO, TD, JP, DL (Director, Eastern Counties Building Society 1972-1974)
1974-1980	Ald. G. W. Pipe, JP (Director, Eastern Counties Building Society 1942-1974)
1974-1980	Donald Gould, FCBSI (Director, Eastern Counties Building Society 1962-1974)
1974-1975	M. J. Slater, FRIBA (Director, Eastern Counties Building Society 1943-1974)
1974-1975	L. A. E. Stevens, MBE, FRICS (Director, Eastern Counties Building Society, 1947-1974)

Principal Executives

Managing Directors

1869-1913	Thomas Shaw
1913-1929	Arthur H. Shaw
1962-1969	Sir Hubert Newton, Hon. MA (Keele), FCIS, FCBSI
1966-1968	Edward Moody, FCCS, FCBSI
1977-1984	Norman Cowburn, FCIS, FCBSI
1980-1981	John Quipp, ACBSI
1985-	Michael Shaw, FCA

Chief General Managers

1969-1970	W. G. Hardy, LLB, MBIM, MIOM
1970-1976	Norman Cowburn, FCIS, FCBSI
1982-1985	Michael Shaw, FCA

General Managers

1941-1965	Hubert Newton, FCIS, FCBSI
1966-1970	Norman Cowburn, FCIS, FCBSI
1966	Edward Kempson
1970-1976	John Quipp, ACBSI
1974-1976	John Sharman (East Anglia)
1977-1981	Michael Shaw, FCA
1979-	John Yewdall, FCIS, ACBSI
1985-	J. Roy Griffiths, FBIM (Development)
1985-	Ken T. Heywood, FBIM (Administration)

Secretaries

1856-1869	Thomas Shaw
1869-1873	William Brough
1874-1909	Thomas Brealey
1909-1933	Francis Billing
1933-1963	Hubert Newton, FCIS, FCBSI
1963-1967	Leslie Beardmore, FCBSI
1963-1965	Norman Cowburn, FCIS, FCBSI
1966-1970	J. C. Chaplin, FCBSI
1968-1984	John Yewdall, FCIS, ACBSI
1985-	Roy G. Hewson, FCIS, FCBSI

Accountants

1894-1909	Francis Billing
1918-1933	Harry Ind

Chief Accountants

1956-1974	John Webb, FCCA, FCBSI
1975-1976	Michael Shaw, FCA (1967-1974 Eastern Counties Building Society)
1985-	Trevor Bayley, FCA

Steward and Ex-officio Director

1895-1922	William Johnson

Appendix 2

OFFICES

Head Offices

LEEK: P.O. Box 20, Newton House, Leek, Staffs., ST13 5RG.
Telephone 0538 LEEK 385131

IPSWICH: P.O. Box 35, Queen's House, Ipswich, IP1 1SP,
Telephone 0473 IPSWICH 55866

Regional Boards

East Anglia	The Hon. Peter Strutt, MC
London	D. Berriman, MA, FIB, CBIM
	John Hill, MA, C.Eng, MI, MECH E, MIMC
	E. W. Wallaker, FSVA
North Staffs	John Quipp, ACBSI
	Norman Cowburn, FCIS, FCBSI
	The Earl of Shrewsbury and Waterford
South West	J. R. Robinson, FCBSI

Consultant Director for Wales
A. M. Rees, CBE, K.St.J., QPM, DL, MA

Area Board

Colne (Lancs)
J. C. Holt
J. Downey
C. M. Thomas
J. G. Whittle

Local Boards

Bath
A. J. B. Taylor
T. A. Wyatt

Calne (Wilts)
J. G. Hunt

Denton (Lancs)
D. G. Birtwistle
H. Hardy

Driffield (Yorks)
R. M. H. Beston
S. B. Butterworth
D. Howard
H. T. Leason

Northern
F. Aston
E. Green
A. Cross
L. Shield

Pontypridd (Mid Glamorgan)
D. J. R. Evans
R. Griffiths
J. Phillips
R. L. Prior
J. B. Williams

South Wales
I. G. Cleaver
J. A. Meyrick Owen

Wellington (Somerset)
C. J. Edhouse
E. I. C. Edhouse
V. D. C. Farrant
T. H. Harding
C. R. Wharton

West of England
G. Casey

West Midlands
A. J. Hadlington

Regional Managers

	Telephone
East Anglia A. E. Burroughs 171a Felixstowe Road, Ipswich, Suffolk, IP1 1SP	0473 721158
London M. Bushe, ACIS 60 Kingsway, London WC2B 6DS	01-405 4451
Midlands (East) W. D. Eardley, FAAI, FCBSI Trinity Walk, Off Upper Parliament Street, Nottingham NG1 2AN	0602 472880
Midlands (West) C. J. Bonsall, FBIM 1 King Street, Newcastle, Staffs, ST5 1EX	0782 621965
North East J. G. Fenton, FSVA 47 Hustlergate, Bradford, Yorks, BD1 1PH	0274 735142
North West N. J. Rushton, MBIM 10 London Road, Alderley Edge, Cheshire SK9 7JS	0625 583944
Southern N. M. Hornsey 204 High Street, Guildford, Surrey, GU1 3HZ	0483 61958
South West K. Mullins, ACII, FCBSI 10a Princesshay, Exeter, Devon, EX1 1NA	0392 51072

Scottish Office
7/9 Cadzow Street, Hamilton, ML3 6EE
Telephone 0698 283970

Manager for
Scotland
A. M. Bell

NALGO Office
London: 1 Mabledon Place, London, WC1H 9AN

Telephone 01-388 7591

Appendix 3

THE BRITANNIA FAMILY

1856		LEEK AND MOORLANDS FOUNDED
Formal date of merger		SOCIETY
1938	1.10.38	LONGTON MUTUAL PERMANENT BENEFIT
1953	1. 2.53	ASHFORD PERMANENT (Westbourne Park) RAILWAY PERMANENT (Westbourne Park)
1956	1. 1.56	NORTH STAFFORDSHIRE PERMANENT ECONOMIC BENEFIT
1957	1. 8.57	STONE NEW FREEHOLD BENEFIT
	31.12.57	NEWCASTLE-UNDER-LYME BENEFIT
1958	31.12.58	NEWCASTLE AND DISTRICT
1959	30. 4.59	SOUTHDOWN PERMANENT
	1.10.59	SILSDEN
1960	1. 7.60	NALGO
	30. 9.60	STOCKPORT ATLAS
1961	30. 6.61	RADCLIFFE
	30. 9.61	CONGLETON EQUITABLE BENEFIT
	31.12.61	STOCKPORT AND EAST CHESHIRE
1964	1. 1.64	KIDDERMINSTER MUTUAL BENEFIT
	1. 4.64	AYLESBURY PERMANENT
	1. 7.64	LION
1965	1. 1.65	LLOYDS PERMANENT (Westbourne Park)
	8.11.65	PENISTONE
	31.12.65	WESTBOURNE PARK – CHANGE OF NAME TO LEEK AND WESTBOURNE
1966	1. 1.66	ORIENT PERMANENT
	1. 3.66	CREWE PERMANENT BENEFIT
	31.10.66	LONGDENDALE PERMANENT BENEFIT
	1.11.66	GLOSSOP PERPETUAL
1967	31. 3.67	NATIONAL INDEPENDENT PERMANENT BENEFIT
	1. 5.67	ACME
	1.11.67	GREATER LONDON PERMANENT

1968	1. 1.68	GLOBE
	1. 1.68	ALLIANCE PERPETUAL
	1. 6.68	SUMMIT
	31. 8.68	PEMBROKESHIRE PERMANENT BENEFIT
	31. 8.68	FENTON MUTUAL PERMANENT BENEFIT
1969	1. 1.69	TOWN AND COUNTRY PERMANENT BENEFIT
	1. 4.69	ST. HELENS AND RAINFORD
1970	1. 1.70	STOCKPORT VICTORIA AND REDDISH
	1. 3.70	KESWICK
1971	30. 4.71	WEARSIDE
	1. 6.71	TUNSTALL
1972	1. 1.72	QUEEN ANNE
	1. 1.72	NEW HOMES
1973	1. 6.73	PARAMOUNT
1974	1. 5.74	EASTERN COUNTIES – CHANGE OF NAME TO LEEK WESTBOURNE AND EASTERN COUNTIES
	1. 7.74	OLDBURY BRITANNIA
1975	1. 1.75	CONSETT RELIANCE
	31. 3.75	CITY OF CARDIFF
	1. 7.75	BATH LIBERAL
	1.11.75	CHESTERFIELD BENEFIT
	28.12.75	BRITANNIA – CHANGE OF NAME
1977	1.10.77	CALNE AND DISTRICT PERMANENT BENEFIT
	1.11.77	WESTBURY AND DISTRICT PERMANENT
1978	1. 4.78	THE GLANTAWE PERMANENT
1980	1.11.80	STOKE-ON-TRENT PERMANENT
1981	30. 4.81	ALFRETON
1982	31. 3.82	WELLINGTON (SOMERSET)
	30. 4.82	DENTON
	30. 6.82	OVER DARWEN
	31.10.82	DRIFFIELD
1983	1. 4.83	COLNE
	1. 5.83	WELSH ECONOMIC

Appendix 4

PROGRESS SINCE 1856

NUMBER OF MEMBERS

Year	
1857	203
1863	637
1866	925
1868	1,153
1880	1,756
1885	1,956
1890	2,351
1895	2,642
1900	3,641

Early Balance Sheets Showed Total Number of Members Only

NUMBER OF ACCOUNTS

Year	Shareholders	Depositors	Borrowers	Total
1906	3,693	10	729	4,432
1916	4,626	5	942	5,573
1926	10,339	20	3,254	13,613
1931	15,395	9	5,558	20,962
1936	19,603	575	11,053	31,231
1941	19,928	1,235	14,115	35,278
1946	22,914	1,315	16,510	40,739
1951	28,803	1,774	22,524	53,101
1956	42,829	2,358	30,111	75,298
1961	83,939	4,387	46,184	134,510
1966	192,061	8,709	84,861	285,631
1971	315,269	7,627	107,424	430,320
1976	551,299	9,120	132,625	693,044
1981	918,756	11,326	153,813	1,083,895
1982	1,014,808	11,502	158,207	1,184,517
1983	1,085,850	12,456	164,850	1,263,156
1984	1,138,078	13,065	174,339	1,325,482

Appendix 5

PROGRESS SINCE 1856

Year	Advanced During the Year	Total Assets		Reserves
	£	£		£
1857	3,000		Early Balance Sheets Showed Receipts and Payments Only	
1863	12,673			706
1866	9,317	40,215	Division Between Mortgages, Shareholders and Depositors Not Shown in Early Balance Sheets	905
1868	13,748	48,886		1,369
1872	12,730	80,549		2,366
1875	24,616	125,991		3,376
1880	23,663	193,660		7,709
1885	15,261	220,000		11,581
1890	45,199	250,000		19,788
1895	45,285	331,000		26,525
1900	66,072	460,000		36,006

Year	Advanced During the Year	Total Assets	Mortgages	Shareholders	Depositors	Reserves
	£	£	£	£	£	£
1906	72,707	594,693	559,632	541,002	6,347	44,309
1911	80,685	673,831	612,131	618,164	—	53,342
1916	25,162	713,437	626,489	657,843	2,850	49,542
1921	252,675	1,167,908	1,012,347	1,055,096	38,228	69,000
1926	384,632	2,075,883	1,845,656	1,911,958	19,533	140,337
1931	656,863	3,383,426	3,049,013	3,149,334	14,826	211,042
1936	1,206,391	5,379,900	4,966,591	4,482,465	565,859	312,252
1941	218,103	7,086,433	5,886,495	5,848,671	794,317	427,500
1946	3,794,733	11,113,959	9,031,232	9,538,621	899,842	603,781
1951	5,166,630	21,410,387	19,452,922	17,794,800	2,528,017	907,212
1956	5,002,324	36,057,062	29,973,474	31,513,980	2,643,929	1,591,517
1961	9,855,464	68,590,978	56,384,622	61,113,551	3,456,032	3,330,326
1966	28,062,689	195,942,813	152,041,54	173,848,889	7,229,388	9,706,955
1971	65,948,510	349,123,263	261,290,30	317,555,982	9,493,541	16,936,654
1976	155,794,249	781,249,011	575,988,45	714,705,582	17,062,104	31,311,601
1981	331,946,750	1,675,536,509	1,266,609,978	1,532,360,443	28,370,081	64,303,303
1982	385,505,701	1,995,166,856	1,488,039,367	1,826,886,139	30,047,452	81,542,462
1983	459,511,579	2,376,351,898	1,756,627,033	2,061,458,168	157,760,028	106,234,239
1984	622,669,719	2,847,042,701	2,141,443,714	2,421,603,194	236,958,377	122,698,292

1983 and 1984 Depositors figures include Sterling Certificates of Deposits and Time Deposits.

INDEX